Jane's
POCKET GUIDE
MODERN MILITARY
HELICOPTERS

TIM RIPLEY

HarperCollins*Publishers*

Contents

Contents

Introduction

"Death from Above" was the famous insignia on the nose of Lieutenant Colonel Kilgore's UH-1 Huey gunship in Francis Ford Coppola's Vietnam War epic *Apocalypse Now*. The 25-minute long section of the movie where the 1/9th 'Air Cav' take a Vietcong-held village to the sound of Wagner's *Ride of the Valkyries* captured perfectly the essence of going to war by helicopter.

Since the Vietnam War the helicopter has been an integral part of every armed force, and rotary-winged aircraft have seen action in every major conflict and many small wars. This rapid acceptance of helicopters into the mainstream of military organisations in attack, reconnaissance, liaison, transport, medical and maritime roles has led one commentator to term them 'rotary-winged fighting vehicles'.

However, when helicopters first saw action during the Korean War, they were used by US armed forces for casualty evacuation and VIP transport only. Indeed, it was left to the French to first demonstrate the combat potential of the armed helicopter during their colonial conflict in Algeria. The 1950s and 60s also coincided with revolutionary developments in helicopter design, such as the tandem rotor and turboshaft powerplants.

The success of US Army and Marine Corps gunships in Vietnam spurred the Soviet, British, French, Italian, Israeli, German and numerous other armed forces to field their own fleets of helicopters for anti-tank and assault work. By the mid-1970s most armies had began programmes to procure specialist attack helicopters, leading to the development of the current generation of Cobras, Apaches, Tigers, A 129s, Mi-24s, Ka-50s and Rooivalks. It must be duly noted that these developments were often made in the face of stiff opposition from air force 'blue suiters', who saw the armed helicopter as a direct rival to their own fleets of fixed-wing close air support aircraft.

No such argument was put forward by the navies of the world, however, as they had been quick to embrace the armed helicopter for the anti-submarine and anti-surface vessel roles, as well as more conventional air transport duties.

Indeed, the 1982 Falklands War proved the worth of the helicopter in naval warfare, protecting the British fleet from Argentine submarine attack, decoying Exocet missiles with electronic jamming devices and sinking enemy shipping with guided missiles. Five years later US Army and Navy helicopters provided vital protection against Iranian fast patrol boats in Persian Gulf.

The 1991 Gulf War saw helicopters employed successfully in a wide range of roles by Coalition forces, whilst in the aftermath of the conflict, multi-national relief efforts to help Kurdish refugees in Northern Iraq depended on helicopters to fly in supplies to remote mountain camps.

In the post-Cold War world, humanitarian aid and peacekeeping missions have seen ostensibly military helicopters put to extensive use. Media images of United Nations relief operations in Somalia, Haiti, Rwanda, Bosnia and elsewhere are dominated by swarms of helicopters. NATO peace enforcing missions in Bosnia have seen the Apache attack helicopter intimidating local forces into keeping the peace.

From a communist standpoint, Soviet forces used helicopter gunships to great effect during their long conflict in Afghanistan from 1979 onwards. The simple, but rugged, Mil Mi-8 and Mi-24 assault helicopters became familiar images on snatched footage shot by western television crews cowering with the Mujhadeen guerrillas at the bottom of parched Afghan valleys. In 1994 Russian helicopters were again in action against Islamic guerrillas in Chechnya. Combat helicopters from the former Soviet Union are much in demand because of their low cost and reliability. Proof of this has come very recently when, in a remarkable vote of faith in their former opponents' equipment, the South African-based mercenary organisation Executive Outcomes has become a regular user of Mi-8 and Mi-24s during its operations in Angola and Sierra Leone.

This Jane's guide aims to describe the major combat helicopters in service today, or in the final stages of development. We have classified combat helicopters as rotary-winged aircraft designed specifically for military use, or civilian machines adopted for use by military forces.

Increasingly, armed forces are making use of chartered civilian helicopters as a means to cut costs, and we have enclosed the types used by contractors in this study, particularly those chartered by the United Nations for humanitarian and peacekeeping missions.

We also take note of a number of major changes in the helicopter industry. For example, the consolidation of helicopter manufacturers into a smaller number of larger companies is reflected in the usage of new company titles. We have, however, included details of what are termed 'heritage companies' for reference. As a rule, we have used the current name of the manufacturer, or last name manufacturer before production ceased.

The opening up of the Russian defence industry since the demise of the Soviet Union has meant that it is now possible to attribute long-established designs to their real manufacturers, rather than just link products to design bureau (known as OKB). Actual Russian helicopter and weapon designations are also used to supplement NATO reporting names.

Helicopter production continues around the world in large numbers in spite of the general down turn in global defence spending. This trend will continue as combat helicopters continue to be in the forefront of military thinking and actual operations well into the 21st Century. New technical developments such as the introduction of tilt rotors and advanced compound helicopters also offer military helicopter users significant improvements in both performance and operational capabilities.

Tim Ripley

Lancaster, October 1997

Aerospatiale Alouette II (France)

Type: Light helicopter   **Accommodation:** One pilot; four passengers

Development/History
After it first flew in 1955, the Alouette II became the world's first turboshaft powered helicopter to enter production.

Variants
SE 3130: Two prototype Alouette IIs, powered by the 268 kW (360 shp) Turboméca Artouse I turboshaft.
SE 313B: Designation after Sud-Est merged with Quest Aviation in 1957, later re-named Sud-Aviation.
SE 3140: Alouette II development powered by a 298 kW (400 shp) Turboméca Turmo II engine, but none produced.
SA 3180: Alouette II derivative powered by the more economical Aztazou IIA with a new centrifugal clutch.
SA 318C: Production version of SA.3180.
SA 315B Lama: Powered by Turboméca Artouste IIIB. Assembled in India (Cheetah) and Brazil (HB 315B Gaviao).

Status
French production ended 1975. Indian production continues.

Operators
Argentina, Belgium, Benin, Bolivia, Cameroon, Chile, Congo, Ecuador, El Salvador, Dominican Republic, Germany, Guinea-Bissau, India, Lebanon, Namibia, Senegambia, Togo, Tunisia.

Manufacturers
Sud-Est/Sud-Aviation/Aerospatiale (France), Hindustan Aeronautics Ltd (India), Helibras(Brazil), Saab (Sweden), Republic Aviation (USA).

Aerospatiale Alouette II   (Tim Ripley)

Specifications (for SA 318C)

Powerplant
One Turboméca Astazou IIA turboshaft
Power: 530 shp (395 kW) de-rated to 360 shp (268kW)

Dimensions
Length: 39 ft 8 in (12.10 m)
Rotor diameter: 33 ft 5.6 in (10.20 m)
Height: 9 ft (2.75 m)

Weights
Empty: 1961 lb (890 kg)
Max T/O: 3638 lb (1650 kg)
Payload: 1323 lb (600 kg)

Performance
Max speed: 127 mph (205 kmh)
Range: 388 nm (720 km)

Armament
AS11 and 12 wire-guided anti-tank missiles; free-flight rockets; machine guns

Aerospatiale Alouette III (France)

Type: Light helicopter   **Accommodation:** Two pilots, five passengers

Development/History

The best-selling Alouette III grew out of the smaller Alouette II. The first prototype flew in 1959 and rapidly became a best-selling machine with 2,262 built and 74 countries operating the helicopter at the height of its popularity. Originally intended for service with the French armed forces in Algeria, that conflict came to an end before it was in widespread use. Portuguese, Rhodesian and South African forces used the helicopter extensively in their long bush wars with Nationalist guerrillas throughout Southern Africa. It has been used extensively in conflicts on the Indian sub-continent by Indian and Pakistani forces, performing well in the high Himalayas. Versions have been used for liaison, observation, attack, assault transport, anti-submarine warfare, anti-surface warfare, anti-armour, combat search and rescue, counter-insurgency and armed reconnaissance work.

Sud-Aviation, later Aerospatiale, were keen to use license production deals to foster business relationships in the Eastern Bloc and Third World. They were one of the first western aviation companies to offer technology transfer and work on the Alouette family helped establish the Indian, Romanian and South African helicopter industries.

Variants

SE 3160: Alouette III powered by one 649 kW (870 shp) Turboméca Artouste IIIB turboshaft, de-rated to 410 kW (550 shp).
SA 316A: Production version of SE 3160.
SA 316B: Featured strengthened main and tail rotor to allow

Aerospatiale Alouette III   *(Tim Ripley)*

Specifications (for SA 319B)

Powerplant
One Astazou XIV turboshaft
Power: 870 shp (649 kW) de-rated to 600 shp (447 kW)

Dimensions
Length: 33 ft 4 in (10.2 m)
Rotor diameter: 36 ft 1 in (11 m)
Height: 9 ft 9 in (2.9 m)

Weights
Empty: 2436 lb (1105 kg)

Max T/O: 4630 lb (2100 kg)
Payload: 1650 lb (750 kg)

Performance
Max speed: 136 mph (220 kmh)
Range: 325 nm (605 km)

Armament
AS12 guided missiles; Mk.44 ASW torpedoes; machine guns (pod or door mounted); free-flight rocket pods

Aerospatiale Alouette III (France)

Aerospatiale Alouette III of Royal Netherlands Air Force (Tim Ripley)

Mauser canon in cabin known as K-Car.

IAR-317 Skyfox: Prototype Romania gunship version, armed with anti-tank missiles, free-fall rockets and machine gun pods which did not enter production.

Atlas Aviation XH-1 Alpha: South Africa weapon system demonstrator for Rooivalk attack helicopter.

Status

Production in France ceased in 1983 after 1455 built. Some 230 built in Romania until 1989. Limited production continued only in India, with 300 built to date.

Operators

Algeria, Angola, Argentina (navy), Austria, Belgium (navy), Burkina Faso, Burundi, Cameroon, Chad, Congo Republic, Ecuador (air force), Equatorial Guinea, France (army/navy/air force), Ghana, Greece (navy), Guinea, Guinea-Bissau, India (army/navy), Iraq, Ireland, Jordan, Lebanon, Libya, Malaysia (army), Mexico (navy), Morocco, Mozambique, Myanmar, Namibia, Nepal, Netherlands, Nicaragua, Pakistan (army/navy/air force), Peru (army/navy/air force), Portugal, Romania, Rwanda, South Africa, Suriname, Switzerland, Togo, Tunisia, UAE (Abu Dhabi), Venezuela (army), Congo (former Zaire) and Zimbabwe.

Manufacturers

Sud-Aviation/Aerospatiale (France), ICA Brasov (Romania), Federal Aircraft Factory (Switzerland) and Hindustan Aeronautics Ltd (India).

for greater performance. Produced in Romania as IAR-316B and in India as Chetak.

SA 316C: Artouste IIID powered variant built in limited numbers.

SA 319B: Direct development of the SA 316B, powered by a more efficient and more economical 649 kW (870 shp) Turboméca Astazou XIV turboshaft, de-rated to 447 kW(660 shp).

G-Car: Rhodesian Air Force gunship versions with two side-mounted Browning machine guns. Gunship with single port firing 20 mm

Aerospatiale Super Frelon (France)

Type: Heavy lift helicopter   **Accommodation:** Two pilots, up to 37 passengers

Development/History
First flown in the 1962 to meet French Navy requirements
for a maritime helicopter armed with anti-ship guided
missiles and ASW weapons. Some remain in French service
for logistic support and vertical replenishment at sea.

Variants
SA 321: Pre-production aircraft
SA 321G: French ASW version, later able to fire Exocet
SA 321Ga: French navy cargo carrying and assault transport.
SA 321GM: Export version for Libya.
SA 321F: Civilian version.
SA 321H: Version sold to Iraq with Turmo IIIE engines,
Omera ORB-31D radar and Exocet missiles.
SA 321J & Ja: Civilian version.
SA 321K: Export transport version to Israel.
SA 321L: Export transport version to South Africa.
SA 321M: Export transport/rescue version to Libya.
Changhe Z-8: Chinese-built naval and combat version.

Status
Production continues in China only.

Operators
France (navy), China (navy), Iraq and Libya.

Manufacturer
Sud-Aviation/Aerospatiale (France) and Changhe Aircraft
Factory (China).

Aerospatiale SA 321 Super Frelon   *(Tim Ripley)*

Specifications (for SA321G)

Powerplant
Three Turboméca Turmo IIIC turboshafts
Power: 4710 shp (3510 kW)

Dimensions
Length: 63 ft 7 in (19.4 m)
Rotor diameter: 62 ft (18.9 m)
Height: 16 ft 2 in (4.9 m)

Weights
Empty: 15 130lb (6863 kg)
Max T/O: 28 660 lb (13 000 kg)
Payload: 11 023 lb (5000 kg)

Performance
Max speed: 171 mph (275 kmh)
Range: 549 nm (1020 km)

Armament
ASW torpedoes; depth charges; machine guns

Eurocopter Gazelle (France)

Type: Light helicopter   **Accommodation:** One pilot, four passengers

Development/History

Sud-Aviation began work on the Gazelle in the mid-1960s as a replacement for its Alouette family. By 1967 it had been put into the melting pot of the Anglo-French Helicopter Agreement, which was to see the joint development of the Gazelle, Lynx and Puma families of helicopters by Sud-Aviation (later Aerospatiale) and Britain's Westland, This agreement gave France the lead in Gazelle exports, and Aerospatiale was soon leading a major foreign sales drive. Exports and co-production deals resulted in more than 400 sales, 294 being ordered for construction in Britain (all except 12 for the UK armed forces) whilst France bought just under 400. Total production was some 1254.

A year later the Gazelle made its first flight, and soon the version with the revolutionary 'fenestron', or fan-in-fin tail, rotor was airborne. By the mid-1970s the aircraft was in widespread use with the British and French armed forces. From 1973 the French began to field the new SA 342 version, which sported an improved engine. Britain choose not to adopt the new engine for its Gazelles.

British versions saw combat in the Falklands in 1982, but it was in the 1982 Lebanon war that a Syrian version armed with HOT anti-tank missiles showed the Gazelle's true potential as an armed helicopter. French HOT and Mistral missile-armed versions were used extensively during the 1991 Gulf War in the air cavalry role on the extreme left flank of the Coalition forces. 'Free Kuwaiti' Gazelles fought alongside US Marine Corps forces to liberate Kuwait City. Yugoslavian-built versions have been used extensively in armed and unarmed roles during the civil war that broke out

Westland Gazelle AH.Mk 1 of the British Army Air Corps   *(Tim Ripley)*

Specifications (for SA 341)

Powerplant
One Turboméca Astazou IIIA turboshaft
Power: 590 shp (440 kW)

Dimensions
Length: 39 ft 3 in (11.9 m)
Rotor diameter: 34 ft 5 in (10.5 m)
Height: 10 ft 2 in (3.2 m)

Weights
Empty: 2022 lb (917 kg)
Max T/O: 3970 lb (1800 kg)
Payload: 1540 lb (700 kg)

Performance
Max speed: 193 mph (310 kmh)
Range: 361 nm (670 km); 193 nm (360 km) with max payload

Armament
AS11, AS12, HOT, TOW and 9M14M Malyutka (AT-3 Sagger) wire-guided anti-tank missiles; 9M32M Strela (SA-7 Grail) and Mistral air-to-air missiles; Giat M621 20 mm cannon; door- and pod-mounted machine guns; free-flight rockets

in 1991, with Serb-operated Gazelles seeing action against Slovenian, Croat and Bosnia forces.

British and French Gazelles have been used in the former Yugoslavia to support United Nations and NATO peacekeeping forces since 1992. British Army Gazelles operating in Northern Ireland have been fitted with a variety of specialist observation and close circuit television systems.

Variants

SA 340: Two prototypes, first with conventional rotors and T-tail; second fitted with rigid main rotors and fenestron, Astouzou II powerplant of 268 kW (360 shp).

SA 341: Four pre-production helicopters with enlarged cabin, semi-articulated rotors, 440 kW (590 shp) Astazou III and 3968 lb (1800 kg) maximum weight.

SA 341B: British Army Air Corps Gazelle AH 1, 212 built.

SA 340C: British Royal Navy (Fleet Air Arm) Gazelle HT 2, 40 built.

SA 341D: British Royal Air Force Gazelle HT 3, 29 built.

SA 341E: British Royal Air Force VIP transport Gazelle HCC 4, one built and three converted from HT 3s.

SA 341G: Civilian.

SA 341F: French Army Aviation version, 166 built.

SA 341F/Cannon: French Army Aviation M621 20 mm cannon armed version, 62 converted from original Fs.

SA 341H: Initial French military export version.

SA 341H Partizan: Yugoslav-built version.

SA 341M: French Army Aviation HOT armed version, 40 converted from original Fs.

SA 342J: Civilian.

Eurocopter SA 342 L1 Gazelle   (Aerospatiale)

Eurocopter Gazelle (France)

SA 342K: Up-rated military export version with 650 kW (870 shp) Astazou XIVH Powerplant and 4189 lb (1900 kg) maximum weight.
SA 342L: Military export model with improved fenestron. Some 170 built in Yugoslavia, including SA 342L2 GAMA attack and SA 342L2 HERA scout versions armed with Soviet bloc anti-armour and air-to-air missiles.
SA 342L1: Military export version with Astazou XIVM and 4409 lb (2000 kg) maximum weight.
SA 342M Viviane: Final production version for French Army Aviation, with Astazou XIVH and HOT missiles. More than 200 produced. Some 30 fitted with Mistral missile to SA 342M/Celtic standard and later SA 342M/ATAM standard.

Status
No longer in production.

Operators
Angola, Bosnian Serb Republic, Burundi, Cameroon, Croatia, Cyprus, Ecuador, Egypt, France (army) Guinea Republic, Iraq, Ireland, Jordan, Kenya, Kuwait, Lebanon, Libya, Morocco, Qatar, Senegambia, Slovenia, Syria, Tunisia, UAE (Abu Dhabi), United Kingdom (army/navy), Yugoslavia (Serbia/Montenegro).

Manufacturer
Sud-Aviation/Aerospatiale/Eurocopter (France), Westland Helicopters (UK), SOKO (Yugoslavia), Arab-British Helicopter Company (Egypt).

Above:
Eurocopter SA 342M Gazelle for French Army Aviation
(Tim Ripley)

Right:
Eurocopter SA 342 Gazelle fires a HOT wire guided anti-tank missile
(Aerospatiale)

Eurocopter Dauphin/Panther (France)

Type: Light helicopter   **Accommodation:** Two pilots, 10 troops

Development/History

Aerospatiale began development of the Dauphin (Dolphin) as a replacement to the Allouette III in the early 1970s, with the first flight taking place in 1972. The twin-engined version first flew three years later, and it has remained in production ever since, with worldwide sales and a number of licence production agreements being reached. A version with Allison engines entered service with the US Coast Guard in 1987 after a troubled programme to integrate the US-sourced powerplant. Some have since been passed on to Israel. From 1986 onwards, military versions have been christened the Panther, with designations in the 565 series adopted simultaneously. The Dauphin/Panther has proven to be a versatile and reliable light helicopter, which looks set to remain in production and service until well into the next century.

Eurocopter SA 366/HH-65 Dauphin   (IDF Spokesman)

Variants

AS 360: Initial prototype powered by single Turboméca Astazou XVI powerplant.

AS 361H: Initial military version powered by single Turboméca Astazou XVIIIA powerplant.

AS 365C Dauphin 2: Twin-engined version powered by 485 kW (650 shp) Turboméca Arriel turboshaft. In 1990 re-designated as AS 365N2 Dauphin 2. C1,C2, C2 versions.

AS 365N: Improved version with retractable undercarriage.

AS 365N1: Further improvement with 11-bladed fenestron and up-rated Arriel 1C1 powerplant.

AS 365N2: Civil version with Turboméca 1 C2 powerplants.

AS 365K/M: First military version of twin-engined

Specifications (for AS 565 Panther)

Powerplant
Two Turboméca Arriel IMI turboshafts
Power: 1566 shp (1168 kW)

Dimensions
Length: 38 ft 1 in (11.6 m)
Rotor diameter: 39 ft 8 in (12.11 m)
Height: 13 ft 1 in (3.99 m)

Weights
Empty: 4835 lb (2193 kg)
Max T/O: 9369 lb (4250 kg)

Payload: 3527 lb (1600 kg)

Performance
Max speed: 184 mph (296 kmh)
Range: 472 nm (875 km)

Armament
Giat M621 20 mm cannon pods; Mistral air-to-air missiles; HOT wire-guided anti-tank missiles; free-flight rockets; AS15TT and Exocet anti-ship missiles; Murene torpedoes

AS365N2, for attack and troop transport. This was re-named the Panther, powered by Turboméca 1M1 and marketed under the following versions; AS 565AA free-flight rocket and gun armed; AS 565UA utility; AS 565CA anti-tank: AS 365F navalised version with retractable undercarriage: AS 365F1 navalised version; AS 565SA anti-shipping; AS 565MA unarmed rescue; AS 565SC Saudi Arabia rescue.

AS 365N3: Upgraded version with two Turboméca Arriel 2C turboshafts. Panther versions were designated SA 565 UB utility; SA 565 AB cannon/rocket armed; SA 565 MB shipborne utility ; SA 565 SB shipborne armed.

AS 365N4: Civil wide body version, seating 14 and powered by Arriel 2C.

AS 565 Panteras: Brazilian version of K model designated HM-1 by Brazilian army.

Panther 800: Proposed US Army version. Did not enter production.

AS 366G1: Version produced for US Coast Guard under designation HH-65A, with Textron Lycoming LTS1-1-750A-1 engines, specialist night vision and rescue equipment. Also used by Israel.

Harbin Z-9 Haitun: Chinese version assembled from French kits.

Harbin Z-9A-100: Chinese-made version with WZ-8A powerplant, rated to 546 kW (734 shp), which can be armed.

Status

In production in France, Brazil and China.

Eurocopter AS 565 Panther   *(Aerospatiale)*

Eurocopter Dauphin/Panther (France)

Operators

Angola, Bophuthatswana, Brazil (army), Burkina Faso, Cameroon, China, Congo, Cote d'Ivoire, Dominican Republic, Fiji, France (navy, air force), India (air force), Ireland, Israel, Romania, Saudi Arabia (navy), Sri Lanka, Taiwan, Thailand (navy), UAE (Abu Dhabi), USA (Coast Guard).

Manufacturers

Aerospatiale/Eurocopter (France), Helibras (Brazil) and Harbin Aircraft Manufacturing (China).

Eurocopter AS 565F
Panther
(Tim Ripley)

Eurocopter Ecureuil/Fennec (France)

Type: Light helicopter   **Accommodation:** Two pilots, two/three passengers

Development/History

The three-rotor bladed Ecureuil (Squirrel) first flew in 1974 and has remained in production ever since, attracting several thousand military and civilian customers around the globe. The single-engined 350 series version was soon supplemented by the twin-engined 355 series aircraft, which provided greater performance. Since 1990 specialist military versions of the Ecureuil have been marketed under the Fennec (Fox) name, using the series 555 series designation.

Versions

AS 350 Ecureuil: First prototype with single Textron Lycoming LTS 101 turboshaft.

AS 350BA/B2/B3: Civilian/military version with single Turboméca Arriel 1B; B2 with Arriel 1D1; B3 with Arriel 2.

AS 350D: Civilian version with single Textron Lycoming LTS 101 turboshaft. Known as AStar in USA.

AS 350 Firefighter: Specialised version.

AS 350L2: First armed version, powered by 546 kW (732 shp) Turboméca Arriel 1D1, known as Fennec. AS 550C2/C3 anti-tank version. Other Fennec versions include: AS 550U2/U3 unarmed utility; AS 550A2/A3 armed, cannon or rockets; AS 550M2 unarmed naval; AS 550S2 armed naval anti-shipping; AS 550U3/A3/C2 are Arriel 2B powered.

HB 350B/B1 Esquilos: Unarmed Brazilian version, designated CH-50 and TH-50 by Brazilian Air Force, UH-12 by Brazilian Navy.

HB 350L1 Esquilo: Armed Brazilian version, designated HA-1 by Brazilian army.

Squirrel HT 1/HT 2: UK training version of AS 350BB.

Eurocopter AS 355 Ecureuil   *(Tim Ripley)*

Specifications (for AS 350B)

Powerplant
One Turboméca Arriel 1B turboshaft
Power: 641 shp (478 kmh)

Dimensions
Length: 35 ft 10 in (10.9 m)
Rotor diameter: 35 ft (10.7 m)
Height: 10 ft 11 in (3.3 m)

Weights
Empty: 2325 lb (1146 kg)

Max T/O: 4630 lb (2100 kg)

Performance
Max speed: 178 mph (287 kmh)
Range: 394 nm (730 km)

Armament
Giat M621 20 mm cannon pod; 7.62 mm machine gun pod; free-flight rockets; TOW wire-guided anti-tank missiles; Mistral air-to-air missiles; anti-submarine torpedoes

Eurocopter Ecureuil/Fennec (France)

AS 350BA in service with the Australian Army
(API)

AS 355E Ecureuil: First production version with two 313 kW(420 shp) Allison 250-C20F turboshafts.
AS 355N Ecureuil 2: Improved version with two 340 kW (456 shp) Turboméca Arrius 1A. Civil version know as AS 355F2 Twin Star in USA.
AS 355F: Improved rotor blade version.

AS 355F1: French training version. F2 has upgraded transmission.
AS 355M2: French armed version.
AS 555 Fennec: Twin-engined version. AS 555AN armed version with 20 mm cannon; AS 555UN training and utility version; AS 555SR armed naval version; AS 555AR cannon/rocket armed version; AS 555UR utility version; AS 555MR naval utility version; AS 555MN unarmed naval version; AS 555SN armed naval version.
Z-11: Chinese produced copy with WZ-8D Powerplant, rated to 510 kW (685 shp).
AS/HB 555F2: Brazilian version, designated CH-55 and VH-55, or Equilos Bi, by Brazilian air force, UH-12B by Brazilian navy.
Twin Squirrel: UK VIP transport version of AS 555F1.

Status
In production in France, China and Brazil.

Operators
Argentina (coast guard), Australia (army, navy, air force), Benin, Botswana, Brazil (army, navy, air force), Central Africa Republic, Denmark (army), Djibouti, Ecuador(army), Fiji, France (army, navy, air force), Iceland, Ireland, Malawi, Paraguay, Peru (air force), Sierra Leone, Singapore, Tunisia, UAE (Abu Dhabi), UK (air force, army).

Manufacturers
Aerospatiale/Eurocopter (France), Chanqe (China) and Helibras (Brazil).

Eurocopter AS 550 CS Fennec

(Eurocopter)

Eurocopter Puma (France)

Type: Medium lift helicopter   **Accommodation:** Two pilots, loadmaster, 20 troops

Development/History

Work on the SA 330 began in 1963 but the programme became multi-national as a result of the 1967 Anglo-French helicopter agreement. This resulted in Westland building 48 for the British Royal Air Force. Under this arrangement future development and export work on the design was the responsibility of Aerospatiale, later Eurocopter, who began a vigorous sales drive in the 1970s. British and French Pumas have seen action in the 1991 Gulf War and supporting peacekeeping missions in the former Yugoslavia. South African forces used the Puma extensively in their bush wars in Angola and South West Africa. French production ceased in 1987 after 697 built. The design was superseded by Super Puma (Cougar) versions from the late 1970s. The main centres of Puma development are now in South Africa (see Oryx entry) and Romania, where extensively upgraded versions are produced.

Variants

SA 330: First eight French prototypes.
SA 330B: French Army Aviation version.
SA 330C: Military export version.
SA 330E: Royal Air Force version, designated Puma HC 1.
SA 330F & G: Civilian versions with 1174 kW (1575 shp) Turmo IVC powerplant.
SA 330H: Military version with 1174 kW (1575 shp) Turmo IVC powerplant. Designated SA 330B by French air force, even through different from the French army's SA 330B.
SA 330J & L: Uprated G & H versions with glass-fibre rotor blades.

Westland Puma HC.Mk 1 *(Tim Ripley)*

Specifications (for SA 330)

Powerplant
Two Turboméca Turmo IVC turboshafts
Power: 3150 shp (2350 kW)

Dimensions
Length: 46 ft 1 in (14.1 m)
Rotor diameter: 49 ft 2 in (15 m)
Height: 16 ft 10 in (5.1 m)

Weights
Empty: 8303 lb (3766 kg)
Max T/O: 16 315 lb (7400 kg)

Payload: 7055 lb (3200 kg)

Performance
Max speed: 168 mph (271 kmh)
Range: 309 nm (572 km)

Armament
Machine guns; Romanian versions sported free-flight rocket pods; 9M14M Malyutka (AT-3 'Sagger') wire-guided anti-tank missiles; Hull-mounted 20 mm cannons; 220 lb (100 kg) free-fall bombs, A-90 air-to-air missiles

SA 330S: Portuguese versions with ORB 31 radar for maritime surveillance and Makila powerplant.
IAR-330L: Romanian-built version. Systems upgrade underway including installation of SOCAT (Optronic Search and Combat Anti-Tank) weapon package.
Puma 2000: Proposed Romanian version with glass cockpit.
NSA 330: Indonesian-built version.
AS 330B Orchidee: Experimental French test bed for Orchidee ground surveillance radar.

Status

Production continues only in Romania.

Operators

Argentina (coast guard/army), Algeria, Cameroon, Chile (army), Congo (Zaire), Cote d'Ivoire, Ecuador, Ethiopia, France (army/air force), Gabon, Guinea Republic, Indonesia (air force), Iraq, Kenya, Kuwait, Lebanon, Malawi, Morocco, Nepal, Nigeria, Pakistan (army/air force), Philippines, Portugal, Romania, Senegambia, South Africa, Spain, Sudan, Togo, UAE (Abu Dhabi), United Kingdom (air force).

Manufacturer

Sud-Aviation/Aerospatiale/Eurocopter (France), Westland Helicopters (UK), ITPN (Indonesia), IAR SA Brasov (Romania).

Eurocopter SA 330B Puma   *(Tim Ripley)*

Eurocopter Super Puma/Cougar (France)

Type: Medium lift helicopter   **Accommodation:** Two pilots, loadmaster, 25 passengers

Development/History

A 'growth' development of the basic Puma, the Super Puma first flew in 1978 boasting more powerful Makila powerplants. Although aimed mainly at the civilian market, Aerospatiale (now Eurocopter) have marketed specific military versions under the brand name Cougar, using the series 532 designation. Stretched versions with greater seating capacity have been fielded, and a wide range of armament options are available. Recent developments have included a number of night vision options and in-flight refuelling for combat-search and rescue. The French Army are also planning to use the Cougar as the platform for their HORIZON ground surveillance radar system.

Variants

AS 332B1: First military version with Makila powerplants.
AS 332C: First civil version.
AS 332F1: Naval version.
AS 332L1: 'Stretched' civilian version.
AS 332L2 Super Puma Mk 2: Civil transport.
AS 332L2 Super Puma Mk 2 VIP: Civil VIP transport.
AS 355M: Stretched military version, production ceased.
AS 332M1: 'Stretched' military version.
AS 532 Cougar Mk 1: In 1990 B, F and M versions re-designated and the name Cougar adopted for military sales. AS 532AC, UB and UC for short fuselage and military armed/unarmed; AS 532AL and UL for long fuselage, military armed/unarmed; AS 532SC naval, armed anti submarine/anti-ship.

Eurocopter AS 332 M1 Super Puma   *(Eurocopter)*

Specifications (for AS 532UL Cougar Mk 1)

Powerplant

Two Turboméca Makila 1A1 free turbines
Power: 3754 shp (2800 kW)

Dimensions

Length: 50 ft 11 in (15.5 m)
Rotor diameter: 51 ft 2 in (15.6 m)
Height: 15 ft 9 in (4.8)

Weights

Empty: 0516 lb (1030 kg)

Max T/O: 19 841 lb (9000 kg)
Payload: 9920 lb (4500 kg)

Performance

Max speed: 172 mph (278 kmh)
Range: 334 nm (618 km)

Armament

20 mm or 7.62 mm guns; free-flight rockets; naval versions can carry the AM 39 Exocet anti-ship missile or homing torpedoes

Eurocopter AS 532 UL Cougar Mk 1 with Horizon battlefield surveillance system

(Eurocopter)

AS 532 Cougar Mk 2: Stretched version with 1569 kW (2104 shp) Makila 1A2 powerplant. Civilian counterpart designated Super Puma II). In-flight refuelling optional. AS 532A2 armed combat rescue version; AS 532U2 unarmed utility with stretched fuselage; AS 532M naval, armed anti-submarine.

Cougar 100: Reduced capability export version.

AS 532UL HORIZON: Ground surveillance version developed from Orchidee system.

NAS 332B: Indonesian utility designation.

NAS 332F: Indonesian naval designation.

CH-34: Brazilian designation for 332M.

HT.17: Spanish Army designation for 332B

HD.21: Spanish Air Force search and rescue designation.

HT.21/A: Spanish VIP designation.

Hkp.10: Swedish search and rescue designation.

Status

In production in France and Indonesia.

Operators

Argentina (coast guard, army), Brazil (navy/air force), Cameroon, Chile (army/navy/air force), China, Congo (Zaire), Cote d'Ivoire, Ecuador, France (air force/army), Gabon, Indonesia (navy/air force), Iraq, Japan, Jordan, Kuwait, Malaysia, Mexico (air force), Nepal, Netherlands, Nigeria, Panama, Peru (army), Qatar, Saudi Arabia (navy/air force), Singapore, South Korea (air force), Spain (army), Sweden (air force), Switzerland, Thailand (air force),Togo, Turkey (army), UAE (Abu Dhabi), Venezuela.

Manufacturer

Aerospatiale/Eurocopter (France), ITPN (Indonesia) and Singapore models were assembled in country from kits. TAI (Turkey) has signed a deal for co-production.

Eurocopter AS 532SC Cougar
(Tim Ripley)

Eurocopter AS 332A2 Cougar rescue version with in-flight refuelling probe

(Tim Ripley)

Eurocopter BO 105 (Germany)

Type: Light helicopter   **Accommodation:** Two pilots, three passengers

Development/History

This German light helicopter made its first flight in 1967, and by the mid-1970s was in widespread service with the German Army – some 96 light observation and 208 HOT missile armed anti-tank versions were eventually delivered. Delays in the Franco-German Tiger programme mean it will have to soldier on in these roles until well into the next decade. It has been widely exported to civilian and military customers around the world.

Variants

BO 105C: Initial version.

BO 105CB: Basic light observation/utility version.

BO 105CBS: Stretched utility version, with capacity for five passengers.

BO 105CBS: Stretched utility version, with capacity for six passengers. Designated Hkp.9B by Swedish Army.

BO 105LS: Canadian produced version with up-rated Allison 250-C28C powerplant.

BO 105M (VBM): German scout version.

BO 105P/PAH-1: Basic German anti-armour version fitted with six HOT missile tubes.

BO 105P/PAH-1A1: Improved German anti-armour versions with new rotors.

BO 105P/PAH-1 Phase 2: Proposed German night attack version.

BO 105P/BSH: Proposed German escort version with four Stinger air-to-air missiles.

BO 105/Ophelia: Trials aircraft with mast-mounted sight.

BO 105ATH/HA.15: Spanish anti-armour version.

Eurocopter BO 105 CBS   *(Eurocopter)*

Specifications (for BO 105C)

Powerplant

Two Allison 250-C20B turboshafts
Power: 840 shp (626 kW)

Dimensions

Length: 28 ft 11 in (8.8 m)
Rotor diameter: 32 ft 3 in (9.8 m)
Height: 9 ft 11 in (3 m)

Weights

Empty: 2868 lb (1301 kg)

Max T/O: 5511 lb (2500 kg)
Payload: n\a

Performance

Max speed: 149 mph (240 kmh)
Range: 550 nm (1020 km)

Armament

HOT and TOW wire-guided anti-tank missiles;
20 mm Rheinmetal cannon

BO 105GSH/HR/A.15: Spanish armed scout version with 20 mm cannon.

BO 105LOH/HR.15: Spanish observation version.

NBO 105: Basic Indonesian-built version.

NBO 105S: Stretched Indonesian version.

BO 105CBS-5/MSS: Search and rescue/maritime version with surveillance radar.

BO 105 LS A-3: Powered by two Allison 250-C 28C engines. Super Lifter, optimised for under-slung loads.

EC-Super Five: High performance version of CBS for civil market.

Status
In production.

Operators
Bahrain, Brunei, Chile (navy/air force), Ciskei, Columbia (navy), Germany (army), Indonesia (army/navy/air force), Iraq, Jordan, Kenya, Lesotho, Mexico (navy), Netherlands (army), Nigeria, Peru (army), Philippines (navy), Spain (army), Sweden (army), Trinidad, UAE (Dubai).

Manufacturer
Messerschmitt-Bolkow-Blohm/Eurocopter (Germany), ITPN (Indonesia), CASA (Spain), Eurocopter Canada (Canada).

Eurocopter BO 105　　　*(Kentron/Denel)*

HAL Advanced Light Helicopter (ALH) (India)

Type: Light multi-role helicopter   **Accommodation:** Two pilots, 12-14 passengers

Development/History

India's indigenous light helicopter programme was slowed by financial problems throughout the 1980s, delaying the first flight until August 1992. Three prototypes are now flying, but question marks still remain over when it will enter service with the Indian armed forces. The first order for eight was placed in 1997, and the second order is expected in 1998. A production rate of 26 per year is expected from 2002 onwards.

Variants

Army/Air Force: skid landing gear
Naval: wheels and folding tail
Light Attack Helicopter: Proposed gunship version.

Status

In pre-production.

Operators

Nil.

Manufacturer

Hindustan Aeronautics Limited (HAL) (India).

HAL Advanced Light Helicopter   *(Jane's Information Group)*

Specifications

Powerplant

Two Turboméca TM333-2B
Power: 2000 shp (1452 kW)

Dimensions

Length: 42.ft 4in (12.89 m)
Rotor diameter: 43.3ft (13.2 m)
Height: 16ft 3in (4.98 m)

Weights

Empty: 5511 lb (2500kg)
Max T/O: 11 023 lb (5000kg)

Payload: underslung n/a

Performance

Cruising speed: 152 mph (245 kmh)
Range: 496.8 nm (800 km)

Armament

20 mm cannon turret; free-flight rockets; four air-to-surface guided missiles; two air-to-air missiles; mine dispensers; dipping sonar; two homing torpedoes

Eurocopter Tiger (International)

Type: Attack helicopter **Accommodation:** Pilot (front), weapons operator (rear) in tandem

Development/History

Intended to replace the Gazelle in French service and the BO 105 in German service, the Tiger has its origins in a memorandum of understanding signed by the two countries in 1984. After a protracted process, a development contract was signed in November 1989 and work began in earnest to produce five prototypes.

In the early years of the programme both France and Germany were keen supporters of the Tiger, but defence cutbacks in the 1990s have forced the delivery programme to be stretched out, with the first batch of 80 airframes for each country not entering service until the next century (Germany in 2001 and France in 2003). Initially, Germany will receive only UHU close support version, while the French are to receive 70 escort/close support and 10 anti-tank models. Production of the remaining aircraft will then last until 2025, with a total of 215 being built for France and 212 for Germany.

Anti-tank versions are armed with HOT or Trigat anti-tank missiles; a mast-mounted forward looking infra-red sight and air-to-air missiles are also optional. The scout/close support versions are armed with a turret-mounted 30 mm GIAT cannon under the nose, air-to-air missiles and rocket pods.

Variants

HAP Gerfaut: Initial German escort version.
HAP: French escort version.
HAC-3Ggre: French anti-tank version.
PAH-2 Tiger: Initial German anti-tank version.

Eurocopter Tiger   (Eurocopter)

Specifications

Powerplant
Two MTU/Rolls-Royce/Turboméca MTR 390 turboshafts
Power: 2370 shp (1916 kW)

Dimensions
Length: 45 ft 11 in (14 m)
Rotor diameter: 42 ft 7 in (13 m)
Height: 14 ft 2 in (4.3 m)

Weights
Empty: 7275 lb (3300 kg)
Max T/O: 12 787 lb (5800 kg)

Performance
Max speed: 174 mph (280 kmh)
Endurance: 2 hours 50 min

Armament
(HAP) GIAT AM-30781 30 mm cannon; Mistral air-to-air missiles; 68 mm rockets; (PAH-2/HAC) HOT 2/3 wire-guided anti-tank missiles; long-range Trigat infra-red guided anti-tank missiles; AGM-114 laser-guided anti-tank missiles; Stinger or Mistral air-to-air missiles; machine gun pods

UHT: German multi-role close support version, originally designated UHU.
HCP: Export multi-role version, without roof-mounted sight.
U-Tiger: Export anti-tank version.

Status
In pre-production.

Operators
Nil.

Manufacturer
Eurocopter (France/Germany)

Eurocopter Tiger
(Eurocopter)

EH Industries EH.101 Merlin (International)

Type: Shipborne ASW helicopter/utility helicopter

Accommodation: Two pilots, observer, sonar operator

Development/History

This joint British-Italian collaborative programme began in 1979 to develop a Sea King replacement for both countries' navies. Funding was agreed in 1984 to proceed with building nine prototypes and subsequent development. The first prototype flew in the UK in 1987, and since then, the programme has led to the development of dedicated maritime, utility, airborne early war and civil passenger versions. Current order books stand at 44 maritime versions for the British Royal Navy and 22 utility for the Royal Air Force as Wessex and Puma replacement Italy's Navy has ordered eight maritime, four airborne early warning and four utility versions.

Major orders were expected from Canada but the programme was cancelled in 1993 after a change of government. Export orders now being keenly sought from Canada (again), Portugal, Japan and the Middle East. The Merlin programme for the Royal Navy is unique because Westland – the airframe manufacturer – is not the prime contractor. Lockheed Martin is prime contractor, being responsible for integrating the complex anti-submarine sensor and weapon systems with the airframe.

Variants

Merlin HAS 1: Royal Navy maritime helicopter.
EH.101 ASW/ASVW: Italian maritime helicopter.
EH.101 AEW: Italian airborne early warning version.
EH.101 Utility: Italian naval transport version.
Merlin HC 3: RAF support helicopter.
Heliliner: Civilian version.

EH Industries EH.101 Merlin   *(GKN Westland)*

Specifications (Basic Naval version)

Powerplant
Three Rolls-Royce Turboméca RTM 322 turboshafts (UK); General Electric T700-GE-T6A (Italy)
Power: 6936 shp (5172 kW) - 5142 shp (3834 kW)

Dimensions
Length: 74 ft 10 in (22.8 m)
Rotor diameter: 61 ft (18.6 m)
Height: 21 ft 10 in (6.6 m)

Weights
Empty: 15 700 lb (7121 kg)
Max T/O: 28 660 lb (13 000 kg)
Payload: 8598 lb (3900 kg)

Performance
Max speed: 192 mph (309 kmh)
Range: 625 nm (1158 km)

Armament
Mk 46, Sting Ray torpedoes; Sea Skua radar-guided anti-ship missiles; depth charges

EH Industries EH.101 Merlin (International)

CH-148 Petral: Proposed Canadian maritime version.
CH-149 Chimo: Proposed Canadian rescue version.
Cormorant: Proposed Canadian rescue version.

Status
In production.

Operators
Italy (navy), UK (navy/air force).

Manufacturer
Agusta (Italy) and Westland Helicopters/GKN Westland (UK).

Left
EH Industries EH.101 Merlin
(GKN Westland)

Right
EH Industries EH.101 Merlin
(GKN Westland)

NATO Helicopter Industries NH 90 (International)

Type: Multi-role medium-lift/maritime helicopter

Accommodation: Two pilots, (NFH) three systems operators, (TTH) 20 troops

Development/History

This multi-national project began in 1985 and originally involved five nations. However, Britain pulled out in 1987, leaving France, Germany, Italy and the Netherlands to continue building the NATO Frigate Helicopters (NFH) and Tactical Transport Helicopter (TTH). Full scale development began in 1992, and the first prototype flew in 1995. The second prototype equipped with fly-by-wire flight control systems flew in 1997.

Defence cutbacks in Western Europe have led to the programme being scaled down and delivery dates slipped. In mid-1997 the funding for the production delivery schedules was agreed. The Netherlands is taking 20 NFH versions from 2003, Germany wants 205 tactical transports from 2003 and 38 NFH from 2007, France has ordered 27 NFHs from 2005 and 133 TTHs from 2011, and Italy requires 81 NFHs and 143 TTHs from 2004. In total, 647 helicopters are on order, but few commentators expect the programme to survive future European defence budget cuts.

Variants

NFH 90: NATO Frigate Helicopter for shipborne anti-submarine and utility tasks.
TTH: Tactical Transport helicopter.

Status

In production.

Operators

None.

NH Industries NH 90

Specifications (For NFH)

Powerplant

Two Rolls-Royce Turbomeca/Piaggio RTM 322-01/9 or General Electric/Alfa Romeo 700-GE-401X turboshafts
Power: Respectively 4290 shp (3198 kW) or 4800 shp (3578 kW)

Dimensions

Length: 52 ft 10 in (16.11 m)
Rotor diameter: 53 ft 5 in (16.3 m)
Height: 13 ft 10 in (4.22 m)

Weights

Empty: 14 741 lb (6428 kg)
Max T/O: 20 062 lb (9100 kg)
Payload: 4409 lb (2000 kg)

Performance

Max speed: 186 mph (300 kmh)
Ferry range: 650 nm (1204 km)

Armament

Anti-submarine torpedoes; anti-ship missiles; depth charges; 7.62 mm or 12.7 mm door guns

Manufacturer

NHi, with Eurocopter
(France/Germany), Agusta (Italy)
and Fokker (Netherlands).

Right:
NH Industries NH90
(Jeremy Flack/API)

Agusta A 109 (Italy)

Type: light helicopter (for A 109CM) **Accommodation:** Two pilots, six passengers

Development/History
Agusta's stylish light helicopter first flew in 1970 and has sold well around the world since 1975. Armed military versions first entered service with the Italian Army in 1988, although Belgium is the only export customer for this model. To date, more than 576 have been produced in all military and civil versions.

Variants
A 109: Initial production version.

A 109A Mk II: Civil version

A 109C: 'Wide body' version with improved transmission.

A 109EOA: Basic Italian army version .

A 109CM: Current production military versions with sensor weapon improvements.

A 109BA: Belgian Army version with HeliTOW wire-guided anti-tank missiles.

A 109K: Improved transmission and longer nose for more avionics.

A 109K2: Swiss export version.

A 109KM: Fixed undercarriage, with 550 kW (738 shp) Turboméca Arriel 1K1 Powerplant for 'hot and high' operations.

A 109KN: Naval version.

A 109MAX: Medical evacuation version.

A 109GdiF: Coast guard version.

A 109 Power: Two Pratt & Whitney 206C powerplant, each rated to 732 shp (546 kW).

Status
In production.

Italian army Agusta A109   *(Jeremy Flack/API))*

Specifications

Powerplant
Two Allison 250-C20R/1 turboshafts
Power: 900 shp (670 kW)

Dimensions
Length: 35 ft 1 in (10.7 m)
Rotor diameter: 36 ft 1 in (11 m)
Height: 11 ft 5 in (3.5 m)

Weights
Empty: 3509 lb (1590 kg)

Max T/O: 5997 lb (2720 kg)
Payload: Underslung 2000 lb (907 kg)

Performance
Max speed: 193 mph (311 kmh)
Range: 420 nm (778 km)

Armament
TOW-2A wire-guided anti-tank missiles; machine gun pods; free-flight rocket pods; Stinger air to air missiles.

Operators

Argentina (navy/army), Belgium,
Italy (army), Malaysia, Peru
(army), Slovenia, UK (army),
Venezuela (army).

Manufacturer

Agusta(Italy).

Right
Agusta A109 Mangusta
(Tim Ripley}

Agusta A 129 Mangusta (Italy)

Type: Light attack helicopter

Accommodation: Two pilots in tandem

Development/History

Italy's distinctive Mangusta (Mongoose) is the first custom-designed Western European attack helicopter to enter frontline service with a NATO country. With a track record in helicopter construction dating back to 1952, Agusta began working on the Mangusta in the mid-1970s in response to an Italian Army requirement for a specialist anti-armour helicopter.

US experiments with the Cobra and early versions of the Apache obviously influenced the design of the Mangusta, which made its first flight in 1983. Five prototypes were flying by 1986, with a delivery date scheduled for the end of 1987. However, the first production aircraft were not delivered until 1990, with 1.5 being subsequently produced per month. The delay in deliveries was due to funding problems with the Hughes/Emerson/Saab Heli-TOW nose-mounted anti-tank missile sight system.

The initial Italian Army order for 60 aircraft has since been followed by plans to develop a multi-role scout/gunship version. This variant boasts a chin-mounted turret armed either with 12.7 mm (0.50 mm) or 15.5 mm (0.61 mm) machine guns. If a new-build version is not ordered, then 20 of the original airframes may be converted. Despite the A129 seeing combat service with the Italian United Nations contingent in Somalia during 1993, export orders have not been forthcoming – it has lost out in British, Dutch, Malaysian and several Middle Eastern attack helicopter competitions.

Agusta A129 Mangusta　　　　　　　　　*(Tim Ripley)*

Specifications

Powerplant
Two Rolls-Royce 1004D turboshafts
Power: 1650 shp (1230 kW)

Dimensions
Length: 40 ft 3 in (12.3 m)
Rotor diameter: 39 ft (11.9 m)
Height: 11 ft (3.3 m)

Weights
Empty: 5575 lb (2529 kg)
Max T/O: 9039 lb (4100 kg)
External warload: 2645 lb (1200 kg)

Performance
Max speed: 183 mph (294 kmh)
Endurance: 3 hours 5 minutes

Armament
Four hard points; HOT, TOW 2 or 2A wire-guided anti-tank missiles; Hellfire laser-guided anti-tank missile; AIM-9L Sidewinder, Stinger, Javelin, Mistral air-to-air missiles; machine gun pods; free-flight rocket pods: 20 mm Gatling gun chin turret; or 12.7 mm (0.5 in) chin gun tested but not in service.

Variants

A 129: Basic Italian Army anti-tank version.

A 129 Scout: Proposed reconnaissance version with mast-mounted sight and chin gun turret.

A 129 International: Export version with two LHTEC T800 engines, five main rotor blades and improved weapon systems.

A 129 Shipborne: Proposed navalised version.

A 129 Multi-Role: Proposed follow-on to current in-service version, similar in capability to International version, and armed with turret-mounted 20 mm Gatling gun.

Status

In production.

Operators

Italy (army).

Manufacturer

Agusta (Italy).

Right
Agusta A129 Mangusta
(Tim Ripley)

Agusta-Bell AB 212 (Italy)

Type: shipborne anti-submarine helicopter

Accommodation: two pilots, sonar operator radar operator, or seven passengers

Development/History

This specialist anti-submarine version of the popular 412 airframe has become the standard shipborne helicopter for many NATO navies. They are easily identified by the large radar housings above the cockpit and under the forward hull. A variety of surface surveillance radars have been installed, including MEL ARI-5955s, MM/APS-705s or Ferranti Seaspray. Bendix AN/AQS-15B/F dunking sonars have been fitted for anti-submarine work. All weapon carriage is external, with either a mix of anti-submarine torpedoes or anti-ship missiles. Iraqi and Iranian versions saw action during the 1980-88 Gulf War, while Italian, Greek, Spanish and Turkish versions were used to enforce UN sanctions against the former Yugoslavia.

Variants

AB 212 ASW: Basic version.
AB 212EW: Turkish electronic warfare version.
HA.18: Spanish designation.

Status

In production

Operators

Greece, (navy), Iran (navy), Italy (navy), Peru (navy), Spain (navy), Turkey (navy), Venezuela (navy).

Manufacturer

Agusta (Italy).

Agusta-Bell AB 212ASW

(Tim Ripley)

Specifications (for AB 212 ASW)

Powerplant

one Pratt & Whitney PT6T-6 Turbo Twin Pac
Power: 1875 shp (1398 kW)

Dimensions

Length: 42 ft 4 in (12.9 m)
Rotor diameter: 48 ft 2 in (14.7 m)
Height: 14 ft 10 in (4.5 m)

Weights

Empty: 7450 lb (4320 kg)

Max T/O: 11 176 lb (5070 kg)
Payload: 5000 lb (2270 kg)

Performance

Max speed: 122 mph (196 kmh)
Range: 360 nm (667 km)

Armament

AS 12, Sea Killer 2, Sea Skua radar-guided anti-ship missiles; Mk 44, 46 or MQ 44 torpedoes; depth charges. machine guns

Kawasaki OH-1 (Japan)

Type: Light attack and observation helicopter

Accommodation: Pilot, gunner/observer

Development/History

The first military helicopter developed entirely in Japan is intended to replace the OH-6 in Japanese Ground Self Defence Force service in the early part on the next century. A mock up was revealed in 1994, and the first prototype flew two years later. Similar in appearance to the Agusta A 129, but the OH-X features a fenestron tail rotor and 1990s generation materials, sensors and weapon systems. The 1997 defence budget included funding for the first three production aircraft.

Variants
Nil.

Status
In pre-production.

Operators
Nil.

Manufacturer
Kawasaki and Fuji Heavy Industries (Japan).

Kawasaki OH-1

Specifications

Powerplant
Two MHI STI -10 turboshaft
Power: 1318 shp (1768 kW)

Dimensions
Length: 39 ft 4 in (12 m)
Rotor diameter: 37 ft 90 in(11.5 m)
Height: 12 ft 5 in (3.8 m)

Weights
Empty: n/a

Max T/O: 7716 lb (3500 kg)
Payload: n/a

Performance
Cruising speed: 151 mph (260 kmh)
Range: 124 nm (200 km)

Armament
Toshiba Type 91 air-to-air missiles; anti-tank guided missiles; free-flight rockets; turret- and pod-mounted cannon/guns

41

PZL Swidnik W-3 Sokol (Poland)

Type: Medium-lift multi-purpose helicopter   **Accommodation:** Two pilots, 12 passengers

Development/History

PZL Swidnik began to work on upgrading the old Mi-2 design during the 1970s, and the result of that work, the W-3, began test flying in 1979. Production began in 1985, and it has since entered service with the Polish armed forces.

Development to field armed versions is underway, with the help of South Africa and Israel, to improve the export potential of the helicopter by giving customers western and eastern weapons options.

Variants

W-3 Sokol: Standard civil and military version.

W-3L Traszka: Stretched version with up-rated engine to 746kW (1000 shp) and capacity for 14 passengers.

W-3RM Anakonda: Polish Navy search and rescue version.

W-3U Salamandra: Gunship version.

W-3U-1 Aligator: Proposed anti-submarine version.

W-3W: Low cost armed version for Poland.

W-3MV: Proposed naval strike version.

W-3A: Improved avionics version for western markets.

W-3M: As W-3A with floatation bags.

W-3WB Huzar: Armed version upgraded with assistance from South Africa's Denel using the Rooivalk weapon system.

W-3 Salon: VIP transport.

W-3 EW: Proposed electronic warfare version.

W-3 MS/MW: Proposed gunship version with tandem cockpit.

SW-5: Proposed up-engined with Pratt & Whitney PT6C-97B turboshafts.

Specifications (for Sokol)

Powerplant
Two WSK-PZL Rzeszow PZL-10W turboshafts
Power: 1800 shp (1342 kW)

Dimensions
Length: 46 ft 7 in (14.2 m)
Rotor diameter: 51 ft 6 in (15.7 m)
Height: 13 ft 6 in (4.12 m)

Weights
Empty: 7275 lb (3300 kg)
Max T/O: 14 110 lb (6400 kg)
Payload: 4630 lb (2100 kg)

Performance
Max speed: 158 mph (255 kmh)
Range: 661 nm (761 km)

Armament
(W-3U) twin 23 mm GSh-23L cannon pod; 20 mm cannon in nose turret; ZT-3 Grot and Hellfire laser-guided missiles, 9M114 Shturm (AT-6 Spiral) radio- and laser beam-guided anti-tank missiles; 9M32M Strzala (SA-7 Grail) air-to-air missiles; free-flight rockets; mine dispensers

Status
In production.

Operators
Czech Republic, Poland (army/navy/air force), Myanmar.

Manufacturer
PZL Swidnik (Poland).

PZL Swidnik W-3 Sokol
(Tim Ripley)

Kamov Ka-25 (Russia) NATO reporting name 'Hormone'

Type: Shipborne anti-submarine helicopter

Accommodation: Two pilots, (optional) 12 passengers

Development/History
Some 460 Ka-25s were built for service abroad Soviet Navy ships from 1966. It has now been withdrawn from Russian Navy service, but a few are operational elsewhere.

Variants
Ka-25PL: Basic version.
Ka-25F: Proposed land-based attack helicopter.
Ka-25B 'Hormone-A': Original ASW version with search radar, MAD sensor, dipping sonar and sonobuoy launcher.
Ka-25Ts 'Hormone-B': Specialist version to provide target acquisition mid-course guidance for submarine- and ship-launched cruise missiles. Partially retractable undercarriage
Ka-25TL, TI, IV: Missile tracking version.
Ka-25PS 'Hormone-C': Specialist search and rescue version, without anti-submarine warfare equipment.
Ka-25BshZ: Mine warfare version.
Ka-25K: Prototype flying crane.

Status
No longer in production.

Operators
India (navy), Russia (navy), Syria (navy), Vietnam, Yugoslavia (navy).

Manufacturer
Kumertau Aviation (Bashkortostan/Russia) and Ulan Ude (Russia) to Kamov OKB (Russia) design.

Ka-25B 'Hormone-A' on the Minsk   Janes

Specifications (for Ka-25Bsh)

Powerplant
Two Mars GTD-3F turboshafts
Power: 1776 shp (1324 kW)

Dimensions
Length: 32 ft (9.7 m)
Rotor diameter: 51 ft 7 in (15.7 m)
Height: 17 ft 7 in (5.4 m)

Weights
Empty: 10 505 lb (4765 kg)
Max T/O: 15 873 lb (7200 kg)

Performance
Max speed: 130 mph (209 kmh)
Range: 351 nm (650 km) with external tanks

Armament
Anti-submarine torpedoes; depth charges

Kamov Ka-27/28/32 (Russia) NATO reporting name 'Helix'

Type: Shipborne anti-submarine helicopter

Accommodation: two pilots, systems operator

Development/History

The Ka-27 series has a larger fuselage than the Ka-25. The first prototype flew in 1974 ,and it entered frontline service with the Soviet Navy in the early 1980s. Its robust design and rugged construction haven proven popular with crews.

Variants

Ka-27PL 'Helix-A': Basic version for Soviet Navy, also known as Ka-252PL.

Ka-27PS 'Helix-D': Naval search and rescue version.

Ka-27PV: Armed version of PS.

Ka-28 'Helix-A': Export version of PL.

Ka-32S 'Helix-C': Civilian utility and rescue version, with up-graded avionics and search radar.

Ka-32T 'Helix-C': Civil utility version.

Ka-32K: Civil Flying Crane.

Ka-32T: Civil utility version.

Ka-31A1: Fire fighting version.

Ka-32A: Civil version.

Status

In production.

Operators

India (navy), Russia (navy), Vietnam, Yugoslavia (navy).

Manufacturer

Kumertau Aviation (Bashkortostan/Russia) to Kamov OKB (Russia) design.

Kamov Ka-32 'Helix' (Tim Ripley)

Specifications (Ka-28)

Powerplant
Two Klimov TV3-117V turboshafts
Power: 4380 shp (3266 kW)

Dimensions
Length: 37 ft 1 in (11.3 m)
Rotor diameter: 52 ft 2 in (15.9 m)
Height: 17 ft 8 in (5.4 m)

Weights
Empty: 14 330 lb (6500 kg)
Max T/O: 24 250 lb (11 000 kg)
Payload: 11 023 lb (5000 kg)

Performance
Max speed: 168 mph (270 kmh)
Range: 432 nm (800 km)

Armament
Anti-submarine torpedoes; depth charges

Kamov Ka-29 (Russia) NATO reporting name 'Helix-B'

Type: Assault helicopter   **Accommodation:** Two pilots, 16 troops

Development/History

Capitalising on the success of the Ka-27 family, Kamov fielded this specialist assault helicopter version in the late 1980s. It was designed to operate off the Soviet Navy's amphibious landing ships, and is considered to be the 'naval Mi-24', combing firepower with a troop carrying capability.

Variants

Ka-29TB 'Helix-B': Basic assault transport version, also known as Ka-252TB.
Ka-29RLD: Airborne early warning and surface surveillance version, redesignated Ka-31
Ka-27K: prototype anti-submaribe version based on Ka-29 airframe.

Status

In production.

Operators

Russia (navy).

Manufacturer

Kumertau Aviation (Bashkortostan/Russia) to Kamov OKB (Russia) design.

Kamov Ka-29   *(Rosvoorouzhenie)*

Specifications

Powerplant
Two Klimov TV3-117V turboshafts
Power: 4380 shp (3266 kW)

Dimensions
Length: 37 ft 1 in (11.3 m)
Rotor diameter: 52 ft 2 in (15.9 m)
Height: 17 ft 8 in (5.4 m)

Weights
Empty: 12 170 lb (5520 kg)
Max T/O: 27 776 lb (12 600 kg)

Payload: 8818 lb (4000 kg)

Performance
Max speed: 174 mph (280 kmh)
Range: 248 nm (460 km)

Armament
Two 7.62 mm Gatling type machine guns in doors; four hard points; 9M114 Shturm (AT-6 Spiral) radio- and laser-guided anti-tank missiles; free-flight rockets; 23 mm or 30 mm gun pods

Kamov Ka-50/52 (Russia) NATO reporting name 'Hokum'

Type: Attack helicopter   **Accommodation:** One pilot

Development/History

The Kamov OKB has had an interest in attack helicopters since the mid-1960s, when its design lost out to the Mil OKB's Mi-24 in the contest for the Soviet army's battlefield assault helicopter. Kamov resumed work in the 1970s, again with Mil as a rival, to fulfil a requirement for the Mi-24 replacement.

The Kamov Ka-50 first flew in 1982, and won the contest against the Mil's Mi-28 design due to its better agility, heavier armour and firepower. However, the military establishment remained sceptical about the Ka-50's single-seat concept, so work continued on the two-seat Mi-28. First unveiled in public in 1992, the Ka-50 is now being offered for export as the 'Werewolf' or 'Helicopter Soldier', although it has also been called the 'Black Shark' in promotional material.

The collapse of the Russian defence budget in recent years has left Russian army aviation in limbo: neither the Ka-50 nor Mi-28 have entered frontline service, although 12 production versions of the Ka-50 have been completed and work continues on new versions, with a night-attack and two-seater variant flying in prototype form.

The Ka-50 design is revolutionary, with the coaxial rotor allowing the traditional tail rotor to be dispensed with. By going for a single-seat design, Kamov OKB had to incorporate a significant number of automation devices, such as helmet-mounted sight, head up displays and computer navigation devices. Defensive equipment includes self-sealing fuel tanks and armoured engines. The pilot has an ejection seat, which

Kamov Ka-50/52 Werewolf   *(Tim Ripley)*

Specifications (for Ka 50)

Powerplant

Two Klimov TV3-117VK turboshafts
Power: 4380 shp (3266 kW)

Dimensions

Length: 52 ft 6 in (16 m)
Rotor diameter: 47 ft 7 in (14.5 m)
Height: 16 ft 2 in (4.9 m)

Weights

Empty: n\a
Max T/O: 23 810 lb (10 800 kg)
Warload: 6610 lb (3000 kg)

Performance

Max speed: 193 mph (310 kmh)
Endurance: four hours with auxiliary tanks

Armament

One 30 mm 2A42 cannon; 9M120 Vikhr-M (AT-16) laser beam riding guided anti-tank missiles; 9M114 Shturm (AT-6 Spiral) radio- and laser-guided anti-tank missiles; Kh-25MP (AS-12 Kegler) air-to-surface missiles; free-flight rocket pods; 23 mm and 30mm gun pods: R-60M (AA-8 Archer) or R-73 (AA-11 Archer) heat-seeking air-to-air guided missiles

Kamov Ka-50/52 Werewolf/Alligator (Russia) NATO reporting name 'Hokum'

first triggers an explosive device to blow off the rotor blades prior to firing the pilot safely away from the fuselage.

Variants
V.80: Initial prototype.
Ka-50 Werewolf/Black Shark/Helicopter Soldier (unofficially 'Hokum-A')/**V-80Sh1:** Basic single-seat version.
Ka-52 Alligator (unofficially 'Hokum- B') /**V-80Sh2:** Two-seat version.

Status
In limited production.

Operators
Russia (army).

Manufacturer
Progress Arseneyev Aviation Co (Russia) to Kamov OKB (Russia) design.

Kamov Ka-50/52 Werewolf
(Tim Ripley)

Mil Mi-2 (Russia/Poland) NATO reporting name 'Hoplite'

Type: Light helicopter   **Accommodation:** One or two pilots, eight passengers

Development/History

Under Warsaw Pact centralised defence plans, the PZL Swidnik plant was nominated as the sole production site for the Mil OKB Mi-2 design. The first Polish-built Mi-2 flew in 1965, and more than 5200 were built up until production ceased in 1991. The light utility helicopter saw extensive service with Soviet and Warsaw Pact armed forces, including combat operations in Afghanistan and other trouble spots. Civil versions have been licence produced in the USA.

Variants

Mi-2T: Unarmed utility/transport version.
Mi-2U: Dual control trainer.
Mi-2R: Agricultural crop sprayer.
Mi-2S: Medical evacuation version.
Mi-2US Adder: Armed version with 23 mm cannon pod and cabin machine guns.
Mi-2URN Salamandra: Armed reconnaissance version with 23 mm cannon and free-flight rocket pods.
Mi-2URP Anakonda: Anti-tank version with Malyutka guided missiles.
Mi-2URPG: up-gunned version with 9M32 Strela 2.
Mi-2C Chekla: Chemical and nuclear survey and smoke layers.
Mi-2B: Upgraded version with improved electronics for export to Middle East.
Mi-2RM: naval rescue version.
Mi-2Ro: Reconnaissance version.
Mi-2RS: Chemical reconnaissance version.
Mi-2Sz: Dual control trainer.

Mil Mi-2 'Hoplite'   (Tim Ripley)

Specifications (for Mi-2T)

Powerplant
Two Klimov GTD-350 turboshafts
Power: 800 shp (596 kW)

Dimensions
Length: 37 ft 4 in (11.4 m)
Rotor diameter: 47 ft 6 in (14.5 m)
Height: 12 ft 3 in (3.7 m)

Weights
Empty: 5295 lb (2402 kg)
Max T/O: 8157 lb (3700 kg)

Payload: 1763 lb (800 kg)

Performance
Max speed: 124 mph (200 kmh)
Range: 237 nm (440 km)

Armament
Free-fight rockets; gun and cannon pods; 9M14M Malyutka (AT-3 Sagger) wire-guided anti-tank missiles; 9M32 Strela 2 (SA-7 Grail) air-to-air missiles

Mi-2FM: Survey version.
Mi-2D: Airborne command post.
Mi-2 Platan: Mine-laying version.
Umi-2: Reconnaissance trainer.
Variant 51: East German reconnaissance version.
Variant 55: East German maritime version.
Variant 56: East German version
Kania/Kitty Hawk: Version with Allison 250-C20B turboshaft, also known as Kania Model 1.
Spitfire Taurus: US-built version.

Status
Production suspended.

Operators
Bulgaria (air force), Czech Republic, Estonia, Ghana, Guinea Republic, Iraq, Latvia, Libya, Lithuania, Nicaragua, Poland (army/navy/air force), Romania (air force), Russia (army/air force), Slovakia, Syria (air force), Ukraine, USA (army).

Manufacturer
PZL Swidnik (Poland) and Spitfire Helicopter Company (USA) to a Mil OKB (Russia) design.

Left
Mil Mi-2 'Hoplite'
(Tim Ripley)

Right
Mil Mi-2 'Hoplite'
(Tim Ripley)

Mil Mi-6 (Russia) NATO reporting name 'Hook'

Type: Heavy-lift helicopter   **Accommodation:** Two pilots, flight engineer, navigator, radio operator, 65-75 troops, 41 stretchers

Development/History

Mil's giant heavy-lift helicopter made its first flight in 1957, and quickly set new standards in load carrying capacity. The largest helicopter of its generation, the Mi-6 saw widespread service with the Soviet army in Europe and Afghanistan.

Variants

Mi-6 'Hook-A': Basic version.
Mi-6P: Civilian passenger version.
Mi-6T: Military utility version.
Mi-6VKP/VZPu 'Hook-B': Command/EW version.
Mi-6BUS/AYa 'Hook-C': Command type also called Mi-22.
M-6PS: Military rescue version.
Mi-6PZh/PZhz: Fire fighting version.
Mi-6S: Medical evacuation version.
Mi-6Tp: Convertible version.
Mi-6TZ: Fuel transporter.

Status

No longer in production.

Operators

Algeria, Egypt, Ethiopia, Iraq, Laos, Peru (army/air force), Poland (air force), Russia (army), Syria (air force), Vietnam.

Manufacturer

Rostvertol (Factory 168) (Russia) and Factory No 23 (Russia) to Mil OKB (Russia) design.

Mil Mi-6 'Hook'   *(Tim Ripley)*

Specifications (for Mi-6T)

Powerplant

Two Aviadvigatel/Soloviev D-25VM turboshafts
Power: 10 850 shp (8090 kW)

Dimensions

Length: 108 ft 10 in (33.2 m)
Rotor diameter: 114 ft 10 in (35 m)
Height: 32 ft 4 in (9.86 m)

Weights

Empty: 60 055 lb (27 240 kg)
Max T/O: 84 657 lb (38 400 kg)
Payload: 26 450 lb (12 000 kg)

Performance

Max speed: 186 mph (300 kmh)
Range: 540 nm (1000 km)

Mil Mi-8/17 (Russia) NATO reporting name 'Hip'

Type: Medium-lift helicopter   **Accommodation:** Two pilots, optional flight engineer, 24 troops, 12 stretchers

Development/History

The Mi-8 was the work horse of both the Soviet Union's armed forces and their Communist Bloc allies from the mid-1960s. Since the demise of the Soviet Union, the basic soundness of the design, and its low price, has enabled it to carve a major niche for itself in the world helicopter market. Although lacking the avionics of western machines, the glass-nosed Mi-8 combines a useful carrying capacity with the performance to allow it to operate in the most extreme climatic regions.

The Mi-8 first flew in 1961, and has been continually upgraded throughout its long production life. The most significant improvement was the fielding of the up-engined Mi-8MT/TV versions, which was designated Mi-17 for export customers – this version proved its worth in the 'hot and high' conditions experienced during the 1979-89 Afghan war. The bloody conflicts on the fringes of the old Soviet empire and in the former Yugoslavia have seen the Mi-8 employed extensively in European war zones since 1991. The United Nations has also hired numerous Mi-8s to support its peace-keeping and humanitarian operations. To date, some 13,000 have been built for home and more than 60 export customers.

Variants

Mi-8 'Hip-A': Single engined prototype.
Mi-8 'Hip-B': Twin-engined prototype powered by Klimov TV2 turboshafts.
Mi-8T 'Hip-C': Standard production version, powered by two Klimov engines, each rated to 1268 kW (1700 shp). Capable

Mil Mi-8TV 'Hip-H' on UN duty in Croatia   *(Tim Ripley)*

Specifications (for Mi-8MT)

Powerplant
Two Klimov TV3-117MT turboshafts
Power: 3846 shp (2868 kW)

Dimensions
Length: 59 ft 7 in (18.17 m)
Rotor diameter: 69 ft 10 in (21.3 m)
Height: 18 ft 6 in (5.65 m)

Weights
Empty: 14 990 lb (6799 kg)
Max T/O: 26 455 lb (12 000 kg)
Payload: 8820 lb (4000 kg)

Performance
Max speed: 155 mph (250 kmh)
Range: 518 nm (960 km) with auxiliary tanks

Armament
Door-mounted 12.7 mm machine gun; 9M17 Falanga (AT-2 Swatter) and 9M14 Malyutka (AT-3 Sagger) wire-guided anti-tank missiles; 9M114 Shturm V (AT-6 Spiral) radio- and laser-guided anti-tank missiles; 9M120 Vikhr (AT-12) laser beam riding guided anti-tank missile; 9M39 Igla V (SA-18 Grouse) air-to-air missile; free-flight rocket pods

of being armed with free-flight rocket pods. AT/FT Ulan Ube-built versions.

Mi-8PS: Passenger and VIP transport version, also known as Mi-8TP, S or P.

Mi-8TPS: Airborne liaison and command version.

Mi-8MT/TV: Russian military designation for up-engined version with TV3-117MT turboshafts. TV has minor equipment changes. Ulan Ube-built version known as Mi-8AMT/Mi-171. Mi-8 MT/MTV-1/-2/-3 are conversions to Mi-17 standard with port tail rotor.

Mi-8MTV: TV3-117MA powered version, with pressurised cabin.

Mi-8TB/TV 'Hip-E': Armed version with 12.7 mm machine gun in nose and pylon-mounted Falanga missiles.

Mi-8TBK 'Hip-F': Armed export version with six launch rails for Malyutka missiles.

Mi-8TL: Air accident investigation version.

Mi-8R/K: Reconnaissance/Artillery spotting version.

Mi-8MPS: Search and rescue version.

Mi8VZPU or VPK: Airborne radio or command post version.

Mi-8PS 'Hip-D': Airborne command post version.

Mi-8TS: 'Hot & high' desert version.

Mi-9VKP/VzPU 'Hip-G': Airborne command post and radio relay version.

Mi-8SMV 'Hip-J': Communications jammer/ELINT version.

Mi-8PPA 'Hip-K': Export electronic warfare version.

Mi-8PD: Polish airborne command post version

Mi-8MA: Arctic/polar exploration version.

Mi-8MB: Military ambulance versions, also known as Mi-8T sanitarnii.

Mil Mi-8TV 'Hip-H' of the Ukrainian Army Aviation on UN duty in Croatia (Tim Ripley)

Mil Mi-8M 'Hip-H' of Iraqi Air Force

(Tim Ripley)

Mil Mi-17M 'Hip-H'   *(Tim Ripley)*

Mi-8TG: Liquid-methane fuel version, with external tanks.

Mi8-8AMTSh: Night attack and combat rescue version with Shturm and Vikhr guided missiles.

Mi-17 'Hip-H': Export designation for up-engined Mi-8MT/TV/AMT version with TV3-117MT turboshafts.

Mi-17P/PI/PG/PP 'Hip-H(EW)': Export radar jamming version with large fairings for antennas on either side of fuselage. Russian versions designated Mi-8MTSh/MTPSh/MTU/MTA/MTP/MTPB/MTR/MTI/MTPI.

Mi-17Z-2: Czech electronic warfare version.

Mi-17MD: Export version, with TV3-117VM engines, new clamshell rear cargo doors and loading ramp.

Mi-17KF: Export version with new avionics.

Mi-17-1M: High altitude operations version with TV3-117VM engines.

MK-30: Proposed Korean-built Mi-17-1 version.

Mi-17-IV: Military transport and gunship version, with TV3-117VM engines.

Mi-17-1VA: Flying hospital version.

Mi-172 (Mi-17M/V): Export version to Mi-8 MTV-3 standard.

Mi-17P: export passenger version.

Mi-18: Re-used designation for original prototype, new cargo version.

Mi-19: Similar to Mi-9 airborne command post.

Mil Mi-8T 'Hip C' of Croat Air Force seen over Bosnia   *(Tim Ripley)*

Status
In production

Operators
Afghanistan, Algeria, Angola, Armenia, Azerbeijan, Bangladesh, Belarus, Bosnia-Herzegovina, Burkino Faso, Bulgaria (air force), Cambodia, China, Columbia, Croatia, Cuba, Czech Republic, Executive Outcomes (South Africa), Egypt, Eritrea, Ethiopia, Finland, Germany (army), Hungary, India (air force), Indonesia (air force), Iraq, Kazakhstan, Laos, Libya (air force), Lithuania, Macedonia, Mali, Moldova, Mongolia, Mozambique, Mexico (navy), Nicaragua, North Korea, Pakistan (army), Peru (army/air force), Poland (army/air force), Serb Republic (Bosnia), Romania (air force), Russia (army/navy/air force), Sierra Leone, Slovakia, Sri Lanka, Sudan, Syria (air force), Tadjikisitan, Turkey (army) Uzbekistan, Ukraine (army/air force), Venezuela, Vietnam, Yemen, Yugoslavia (air force), Zambia, Georgia, USA (army), United Nations.

Manufacturer
Kazan Helicopter Plant (Tartarstan), Mil Moscow Helicopter Plant (Russia), Progress Arseneyev Aviation Co (Russia), Ulan Ude Aviation Plant (Russia), Daewoo (Korea) to OKB Mil (Russia) design.

Mil Mi-8 AMTSh *(Tim Ripley)*

Mil Mi-17MD *(Tim Ripley)*

Mil Mi-14 (Russia) NATO reporting name 'Haze'

Type: Land-based ASW helicopter   **Accommodation:** Two pilots, sonar helicopter, MAD operator

Development/History

The M-14 is an amphibious version of the Mi-8 developed for the Soviet Navy as a shore-based ASW and rescue helicopter. The first prototypes flew in 1973, and it has since been exported to a number of pro-Soviet states.

Variants

V-14: Prototype.
Mi-14PL 'Haze-A': ASW version with dipping sonar, search radar, retractable search radar and sonobuoy dispensers. The TV3-117 engine, rated to 1417 kW (1900 shp), was adopted during the later stages of production.
Mi-14PLM: Later version with better engines and systems.
Mi-14BT 'Haze-B': Mine-sweeper version produced.
Mi-14PS 'Haze-C': Search and rescue version, with nose search light and anti-submarine gear removed.
Mi-14PX 'Haze-A': Polish rescue training version.
Mi-14 Eliminator III: BT converted to fire bomber.

Status

No longer in production.

Operators

Bulgaria (navy), Cuba, Ethiopia, Libya (navy), North Korea, Poland (navy), Romania (navy), Russia (navy), Syria (navy), USA (army), Yugoslavia (navy).

Manufacturer

Kazan Helicopter Plant (Tartarstan) to Mil OKB (Russia)

Mil Mi-14PS 'Haze-C'   *(Polish MoD)*

Specifications (for Mi-14PL)

Powerplant

Two Klimov TV3-117A turboshafts
Power: 3400 shp (2536 kW)

Dimensions

Length: 60 ft 3 in (18.4 m)
Rotor diameter: 69 ft 10 in (21.3 m)
Height: 22 ft 9 in (6.9 m)

Weights

Empty: 25 900 lb (11 750 kg)

Max T/O: 30 865 lb (14 000 kg)
Payload: n/a

Performance

Max speed: 143 mph (230 kmh)
Range: 612 nm (1135 km)

Armament

Anti-submarine torpedoes; depth charges; door machine guns

Mil Mi-24 (Russia) NATO reporting name 'Hind'

Type: Attack/assault helicopter **Accommodation:** Pilot (rear), weapons operator (front), optional flight engineer, eight troops

Development/History

This distinctive Soviet assault helicopter was developed by Mil OKB in response to American experiences in Vietnam. Sometimes called a 'flying tank' because it was the first attack helicopter to feature heavy armour and be armed with a large calibre cannon. In Soviet/Russian service it is nicknamed the 'hunchback'.

The first prototype made its maiden flight in 1970, but this version boasted a full glass, or 'green house', cockpit, rather than the more-familiar tandem layout of latter models. In 1974 the first production versions were spotted operating with Soviet troops in East Germany, and they were soon in widespread service throughout Eastern Europe.

The invasion of Afghanistan in 1979 gave the Mi-24 its first combat experience, and Soviet pilots soon came to value its heavy armoured protection. Only the arrival of US-made Stinger missiles in the hands of Mujhadeen rebels threatened Soviet air supremacy, so a crash programme to fit defensive systems to the Mi-24 was begun.

With the fall of the Soviet Union, the Mi-24 has seen extensive service in the wars in the Caucasus – Russian Army Aviation used them to spearhead their invasion of Chechnya in 1994. Budget cuts mean Russian plans to replace the Mi-24 have yet to come to fruition, so it will have to soldier on for many years to come. To boost the Mi-24's appeal to export customers, western sensors and avionics have been integrated into the latest new-build versions.

Variants

V 24/A.10 'Hind B': Pre production versions, with TV 2 1117

Mil Mi-24K 'Hind-G2' of the Ukrainian Army Aviation *(Tim Ripley)*

Specifications (for Mi-24P)

Powerplant
Two Klimov TV3-117 series II turboshafts
Power: 4380 shp (3266 kW)

Dimensions
Length: 57 ft 5.5 in (17.51 m)
Rotor diameter: 56 ft 9 in (17.3 m)
Height: 13 ft (3.97 m)

Weights
Empty: 18 078 lb (8200 kg)
Max T/O: 26 455 lb (12 000 kg)
Warload: 5290 lb (2400 kg)

Performance
Max speed: 208 mph (335 kmh)
Range: 540 nm (620 km) with auxiliary tanks

Armament
12.7 mm Gatling type gun or twin 23 mm cannon in nose; 9M17 Falanga (AT-2 Swatter) wire-guided anti-tank missile; 9M114 Shturm (AT-6 Spiral) radio- and laser-guided anti-tank missile; 9M120 Vikhr (AT-16) laser anti-tank guided missiles; 9M39 Igla-V(SA-18 Grouse) and 9A 2200 air-to-air missiles; free-flight rocket pods; 23 mm or 12.7 mm gun pods; twin 30 mm Gsh-30-2 cannon; 30 mm grenade launcher; bombs; chemical weapons; mine dispensers

engines, rated to 1700 shp.

Mi-24A/B 'Hind-A': Original production version with 'green house' front cabin, starboard tail rotor, TV-3-117 engines and Falanga missiles.

Mi-24U 'Hind-C': Unarmed training version of 'Hind-A'.

Mi-24D 'Hind-D': First version to have tandem cockpit, 12.7 mm cannon and Falanga missiles.

Mi-24DU: Dual-control trainer with turret deleted.

Mi-25: Export version of Mi-24D.

Mi-24V 'Hind-E': Introduced radio command-guided Shturm missiles. Powered by TV-3-117A engines. Known as Mi-24W in Polish service. Export version Mi-35.

Mi-24P 'Hind-F': Version of Mi-24D armed with hull-mounted twin 30 mm cannon. Mi-35P export version.

Mi-24VP: Mi-24V with twin 23 mm cannon in nose turret. Mi-35VP export version.

Mi24R, RR, Rkh (Rch) or RKR Hind G: Chemical and nuclear survey/sampling version.

Mi-24K Hind G-2: Artillery fire correction version.

Mi-24VM: Night attack version with western sensor and new titanium rotor head.

Mi-35M: Export night attack version with western sensor, avionics and new Mi-28-style titanium rotor head.

Mi-35U.: Unarmed export trainer.

Mi-24PS: Police/para-military version.

Mi-24E: Environmental research version.

Left: Mil Mi-24V 'Hind-E'   *(Tim Ripley)*

Right: Mil Mi-24V 'Hind-E'   *(Tim Ripley)*

Status

In production.

Operators

Afghanistan, Algeria, Angola, Armenia, Azerbeijan, Belarus, Bulgaria (air force), Cambodia, Croatia, Czech Republic, Executive Outcomes (South Africa), Ethiopia, Finland, Hungary, India (air force), Iraq, Kazakhstan, Laos, Libya (air force), Mongolia, Mozambique, Peru (air force), Poland (army), Russia (army), Rwanda, Sierra Leone, Slovakia, Sri Lanka, Sudan, Syria (air force), Tadjikisitan, Uzbekistan, Ukraine (army), Vietnam, Yemen, Georgia, USA (army).

Manufacturer

Rostvertol (Russia) and Progress Arseneyev Aviation Co (Russia) to Mil OKB (Russia) design.

Left: Mil Mi-24W 'Hind-E' of the Polish Air Force *(Tim Ripley)*

Right: Mil Mi-35 *(Tim Ripley)*

Mil Mi-26 (Russia) NATO reporting name 'Halo'

Type: Heavy-lift helicopter   **Accommodation:** Two pilots, flight engineer, navigator, 80 troops, 60 stretchers

Development/History

Designed to replace the Mi-6, the Mi-26 is the most powerful helicopter in the world. It has a cargo carrying capacity equivalent to that of the C-130 transport aircraft. First flown in 1977, the Mi-26 entered Soviet Army Aviation service in 1985. The UN has chartered a number to support operations in Somalia and the former Yugoslavia.

Variants

Mi-26: Basic version.
Mi-26T: Civil version with D-136 engines
Mi-26MS: Flying hospital version.
Mi-26TM: Planned upgrade.
Mi-26TZ: Tanker.
Mi-26M: Upgraded version with D-137 engines.
Mi-26P: Proposed 70-seat passenger version.
Mi-26TS: Export version.
Mi-26A: Upgraded navigation systems
Mi-26TC: Wide-bodied version with D-136 engines

Status

In production.

Operators

India (army), Peru, Russia (army), Ukraine (army), United Nations.

Manufacturer

Rosvertol (Russia) to Mil OKB (Russia) design.

Mil Mi-26 'Halo'   *(Tim Ripley)*

Specifications (for Mi-26)

Powerplant
Two ZMKB Progress D-135 free-turbine turboshafts
Power: 22172 shp (16534 kW)

Dimensions
Length: 110 ft 8 in (33.7 m)
Rotor diameter: 105 ft (32 m)
Height: 26 ft 8 in (8.2 m)

Weights
Empty: 62 170 lb (28 200 kg)
Max T/O: 123 450 lb (56 000 kg)
Payload: 44 090 lb (20 000 kg)

Performance
Max speed: 183 mph (295 kmh)
Range: 432 nm (800 km)

Mil Mi-28 (Russia) NATO reporting name 'Havoc'

Type: Attack helicopter   **Accommodation:** Pilot (rear) and gunner (front)

Development/History

Superficially similar in appearance to the American Apache, the Mi-28 made its first flight in 1982. Since the aircraft lost the Soviet Army Aviation attack helicopter contest to the Ka-50, the Mi-28 has had a troubled history. The Russian Army Aviation has reportedly been persuaded to place an order for the aircraft, but funding difficulties have so far prevented series production taking place. The aircraft has been undergoing almost continuous development for over 15 years to allow it to fly armed attack missions at very low altitudes. Latest versions on display at western airshows include state of the art night visions sensors and mast-mounted sights.

Variants

Mi-28: Basic version.
Mi-28N: Night attack version with improved sensors and mast-mounted sight.

Status

In low rate production.

Operators

Russia (army).

Manufacturers

Rosvertol (Russia) to a Mil OKB design.

Mil Mi-28N 'Havoc' with rotor mounted sight   *(Tim Ripley)*

Specifications (for Mi-28)

Powerplant
Two Klimov TV3-117VM turboshafts
Power: 4380 shp (3266 kW)

Dimensions
Length: 55 ft 3 in (16.85 m)
Rotor diameter: 56 ft 5 in (17.2 m)
Height: 15 ft 9 in (4.87 m)

Weights
Empty: 15 432 lb (7000 kg)
Max T/O: 25 353 lb (11 500 kg)
Warload: 4000 lb (1814 kg)

Performance
Max speed: 186 mph (300 kmh)
Range: 248 nm (460 km)

Armament
One 2A42 30 mm nose-mounted cannon; 9M39 Igla V (SA-18 Grouse) and 9A 2200 air-to-air missiles; 9M114 Shturm (AT-6 Spiral) anti-tank guided missiles; 9M120 Vikhr-M (AT-16) laser beam riding guided anti-tank missiles; free-flight rockets

Mil Mi-34 (Russia) NATO reporting name 'Hermit'

Type: Light utility helicopter   **Accommodation:** Two pilots, two passengers

Development/History

Designed as a light utility, observation, training and liaison helicopter for military, police, border guard and civil use, the Mi-34 made its maiden flight in 1986. It was the first Soviet helicopter to be capable of executing a loop or roll. Production began in 1993, but funding problems slowed deliveries after six had been built. In 1997 production resumed after a corporate restructuring.

Variants

Mi-34: Basic version.
Mi-34v or VAZ: Twin-engined version, fitted with VAZ-430 twin rotary engines, each rated to 169 kW (227 shp).

Status

In production.

Operators

Russia (air force/army).

Manufacturer

Progress Arseneyev Aviation Co (Russia) and VAZ Motor Car Works (Russia) to Mil OKB (Russia) design.

Mi-34   *(Itar/TASS)*

Specifications (for Mi-34)

Powerplant

VMKB (Vedeneyev) M-14V-26 air-cooled radial engine.
Power: 320 shp (239 kW)

Dimensions

Length: 28 ft 7 in (8.71 m)
Rotor diameter: 32ft 9 in (10 m)
Height: 10 f t (3.2 m)

Weights

Empty: n/a
Max T/O: 2976 lb (1350 kg)

Performance

Cruising speed: 112 mph (180 kmh)
Range: 224 nm (360 km)

Mil Mi-38 (Russia)

Type: Medium lift helicopter   **Accommodation:** Two pilots, 32 passengers

Development/History

Conceived as the replacement for the Mi-8/17 in the medium transport roles, the Mi-38 programme has not really got beyond the prototype stage because of lack of funding. Development began back in the mid-1980s, and a maiden flight was expected for 1993, but did not occur. It bears many similarities to the EH.101 Merlin.

The helicopter has many unique features, including a six-bladed main rotor, a delta 3 type tail similar to the Mi-28's, CRT cockpit displays and extensive use of composite materials. Cargo can be carried under-slung or positioned in the cabin via clam-shell rear doors and a loading ramp. Eurocopter are working jointly with Mil OKB and Kazan Helicopters on the programme.

Variants
Nil.

Status
In pre-production.

Operators
Nil.

Manufacturer
Kazan Helicopter Plant (Tartarstan) to Mil OKB (Russia) design.

Model of the proposed Mi-38   (Paul Jackson)

Specifications (for Mi-38)

Powerplant
Two Klimov TV7-117V turboshafts
Power: 4636 shp (3456 kW)

Dimensions
Length: 64 ft 7.5 in (19.70 m)
Rotor diameter: 64 ft 7 in (21.10 m)
Height: 16 ft 10 in (5.13 m)

Weights
Empty: n/a

Max T/O: 31 966 lb (14 500 kg)
Payload: 11 020 lb (5000 kg)

Performance
Cruising speed: 155 mph (250 kmh)
Range: 700 nm (1300 km)

Armament
Nil

Mil Mi-40 (Russia)

Type: Assault transport helicopter   **Accommodation:** Two pilots, 10 troops

Development/History

Intended as an assault transport version of the Mi-28 attack helicopter. It shares many of the systems of the Mi-28, including engine transmission, main and tail rotors.

Variants:
Nil.

Status
In pre-production.

Operators
Nil.

Manufacturer
Assumed to be Mil OKB (Russia) design.

Model of the proposed Mi-40   *(Paul Jackson)*

Specifications (for Mi-40)

Powerplant
Two Klimov TV3-117MA turboshafts
Power: 4380 shp (3266 kW)

Dimensions
Length: 54 ft 5 in (16.60 m)
Rotor diameter: 56 ft 5 in (17.20 m)
Height: 14 ft 5 in (4.40 m)

Weights
Empty: 16 920 lb (7675 kg)

Max T/O: 25 137lb (11 402 kg)
Payload: 39 681 lb (1800 kg)

Performance
Cruising speed: 183 mph (295 kmh)
Range: n/a

Armament
Anti-tank guided missiles; free-flight rockets; gun pods

Denel Aviation CSH-2 Rooivalk (South Africa)

Type: Attack helicopter   **Accommodation:** Pilot (rear), co-pilot/gunner (front)

Development/History

South Africa's Rooivalk (Red Kestrel) has its origins in an attack helicopter programme that commenced in 1981 in order to develop a successor to the Alouette III gunships then being used in Angola and South West Africa. The South African Air Force has ordered a squadron's worth, but defence cuts have put the order in doubt. Malaysia's new army aviation command may well be the first customer for the Rooivalk.

Variants

XDM: Experimental Development Model.
CSH-2: Basic production model.
ADM: Advanced development model.

Status

In pre-production.

Operators (proposed)

Malaysia (army), South Africa (air force).

Manufacturer

Atlas Aviation/Denel Aviation (South Africa).

Denel Aviation Rooivalk   (Denel Aviation)

Specifications (for CSH-2)

Powerplant

Two Topaz turboshafts
Power: 4000 shp (2982 kW)

Dimensions

Length: 54 ft 7 in (16.5 m)
Rotor diameter: 49 ft 5 in (15.08 m)
Height: 15 ft (4.6 m)

Weights

Empty: 11 618 lb (5270 kg)
Max T/O: 20 723 lb (9400 kg)

Warload: 3022 lb (1371 kg)

Performance

Max speed: 192 mph (309 kmh)
Range: 507 nm (940 km); 720 nm (1335 km) with external fuel

Armament

One 20 mm GA-1 Rattler cannon; ZT-3 Swift, ZT-35 or ZT 6 Mokopa laser-guided anti-tank missiles; V3C Darter or Kukri air-to-air missiles; free-flight rockets

Denel Aviation CSH-2 Rooivalk (South Africa)

Denel Aviation Rooivalk

(Denel Aviation)

Denel Aviation Oryx (South Africa)

Type: Transport helicopter   **Accommodation:** Two pilots, 20 passengers

Development/History

This South African-developed version of the Puma is being aggressively marketed by Denel to users needing helicopters optimised for 'hot and high' bush conditions. In many ways it is similar to the Super Puma because it uses Makila powerplants, but Denel have gone further by modifying the tail section, plus building in the provision for an extensive array of ordnance. Previously known as Gemsbok.

Variants

Option 1: Gun turret version.
Option 2: Side-mounted free-flight rocket launders.
Option 3: Nose-mounted free-flight rocket armament.
Option 4: Anti-armour gunship.

Status

In production.

Operators

South Africa.

Manufacturer

Atlas Aviation/Denel Aviation (South Africa)

Mock up of the stablised sighting system fitted to an Oryx (API)

Specifications (for Oyrx)

Powerplant
Two Turboméca Makila 1A1 free turbines
Power: 3754 shp (2800 kW)

Dimensions
Length: 59 ft 6 in (18.15 m)
Rotor diameter: 49 ft 2.5 in (15 m)
Height: 16 ft 10.5 in (5.14 m)

Weights
Empty: n/a

Max T/O: n/a
Payload: n/a

Performance
Cruising speed: n/a
Range: 303 nm (561.6 km)

Armament
Free-flight rockets; 8 or 16 ZT-3 Swift or ZT-35 laser-guided anti-tank missiles; Darter or Viper air-to-air missiles: 20 mm cannon gun turret

Westland Wasp (UK)

Type: Light general-purpose helicopter

Accommodation: One pilot, three passengers

Development/History
Once the primary shipborne small helicopter of the British Royal Navy, the Wasp is now obsolete and is in the process of being phased out of service by its last remaining users.

Variants
Wasp HAS 1: Shipborne version.

Status
No longer in production.

Operators
Indonesia (navy), Malaysia (navy), New Zealand (air force).

Manufacturer
Saunders-Roe/Westland Helicopters (UK).

Westland Scout AH.Mk 1 *(Tim Ripley)*

Specifications

Powerplant
One Rolls-Royce Bristol Nimbus 503 turboshaft
Power: 710 shp (529 kW)

Dimensions
Length: 30 ft 4 in (9.2 m)
Rotor diameter: 32 ft 3 in (9.8 m)
Height: 11 ft 8 in (3.6 m)

Weights
Empty: 3452 lb (1566 kg)

Max T/O: 5500 lb (2495 kg)
Payload: 1500 lb (680 kg)

Performance
Max speed: 120 mph (193 kmh)
Range: 263 nm (488 km)

Armament
Mk. 46 torpedoes; AS12 wire-guided missiles; Mk 44 depth charges

Westland Lynx (Army version) (UK)

Type: Light multi-purpose military helicopter

Accommodation: Pilot, observer/gunner, 10 troops

Development/History

The British Army's primary light helicopter is another product of the Anglo-French Helicopter Agreement of 1967. Britain's Westland brought Lynx design to the table, and it duly became responsible for its development, production and marketing. Some 113 AH 1s were built for the British Army with skid landing gear, but export sales proved elusive. The British Army Air Corps and Royal Marines/Royal Navy later converted their fleets to armed helicopters (HELARM) by fitting US-made TOW anti-tank missiles. A further 24 AH 9 light battlefield helicopter versions were procured from 1988 to equip 24 Airmobile Brigade.

Variants

AH 1: Original British Army utility version. Some examples armed with TOW missiles.
AH 1GT: Interim armed version until AH 7 developed.
AH 5: Experimental version.
AH 6: Proposed Royal Marines version, not produced.
AH 7: British Army upgraded armed helicopter (HELARM) version with eight TOW missile tubes.
AH 9: British Army light battlefield helicopter version with Rolls-Royce Gem 42-1 powerplant, each rated at 846 kW (1135 shp), tricycle under carriage and BERP rotor blades.
Battlefield Lynx: Proposed export version with provision for Hellfire or HOT anti-tank missiles.
Battlefield 800: Proposed export version with LHTEC T800 engines.
Mk.24/25: Proposed Iraqi export versions.
Mk 02: Proposed Egyptian export version.

Westland Lynx AH.Mk 9   *(Tim Ripley)*

Specifications (for AH 1)

Powerplant
Two Rolls-Royce Gem 2 turboshafts
Power: 1800 shp (1342 kW)

Dimensions
Length: 49 ft 9 in (15.2 m)
Rotor diameter: 42 ft (12.8 m)
Height: 11 ft 6 in (3.5 m)

Weights
Empty: 6040 lb (2740 kg)

Max T/O: 10 000 lb (4535 kg)
Payload: 2000 lb (907 kg)

Performance
Cruising speed: 161 mph (259 kmh)
Range: 340 nm (630 km)

Armament
TOW and Improved TOW wire guided anti-tank missiles; 12.7 mm or 20 mm door or pod mounted machine guns; free-flight rockets

Westland Lynx (Army version) (UK)

Mk 83: Proposed Saudi export version.
Mk 84: Proposed Qatari export version
Mk 85: Proposed UAE export version.
Lynx ACH: Experimental advance compound helicopter with wings for additional lift.

Status
No longer in production.

Operators
UK (army/navy).

Manufacturer
Westland Helicopters (UK).

Westland Lynx AH.Mk 7
(Tim Ripley)

Westland Lynx (Navy version) (UK)

Type: Light multi-purpose naval helicopter

Accommodation: Pilot, observer/gunner, 10 troops

Development/History

Westland's development of the naval Lynx has proved far more success than its effort with the army versions. In addition to the 91 bought by the British Royal Navy, more than 200 have been sold for export, with new orders continuing to be secured.

Armed with the Sea Skua missile, the Lynx proved a potent ship killer both during the Falklands conflict and the 1991 Gulf War. After the Falklands, the Royal Navy began major upgrade programmes to improve the rotor blades, powerplant, sensors, weapon systems and defensive aids. This programme has continued through to the current HAS 8 standard, which is dubbed the Super Lynx.

Variants

HAS 2(FN): French Navy anti-submarine warfare version, with OMERA-Segid ORB 31W radar and Alcatel dunking sonar.

HAS 2: Original British Royal Navy version, with Ferranti Seaspray radar, Bendix dipping sonar and Texas Instruments MAD.

HAS 3: Improved British version with two Rolls-Royce Gem 41-1 kW (shp) engines.

HAS 3ICE: Specialist British version for Arctic operations from HMS Endurance.

HAS 3S: Specialist British version with surveillance and secure communications equipment.

HAS 3GM: Improved British versions for Gulf War with ALQ-167 electronic counter-measures pod and infra-red jammers.

HAS 3CTS: Improved British version with central tactical

Westland Lynx Mk 21   *(GKN Westland)*

Specifications (for HAS 2)

Powerplant
Two Rolls-Royce Gem 2 turboshafts
Power: 1800 shp (1342 kW)

Dimensions
Length: 49 ft 9 in (15.2 m)
Rotor diameter: 42 ft (12.8 m)
Height: 11 ft 6 in (3.5 m)

Weights
Empty: 6040 lb (2740 kg)
Max T/O: 10 000 lb (4535 kg)

Payload: 2000 lb (907 kg)

Performance
Cruising speed: 161 mph (259 kmh)
Range: 340 nm (630 km)

Armament
Mk 44, Mk 46 or Sting Ray anti-submarine torpedoes; Mk 11 depth charges; Sea Skua radar guided anti-ship missile; AS12 wire-guided missiles; 12.7 mm or 20 mm gun pods

Westland Lynx (Navy version) (UK)

systems and flotation bag.

HAS 4 (FN): Improved French Navy version with new Gem 41-1 engine, and gearbox.

Mk 21: Export version for Brazil, designated SAH-11.

Mk 21A: Export version of Super Lynx to Brazil.

Mk 23: Export version to Argentina (later sold to Brazil and Denmark).

Mk 25/UH-14A: Export utility version for Netherlands.

Mk 27/Sh-14B: Export version for Netherlands with sonar.

Mk 80: Export version for Denmark.

Mk 81/SH-14C: Export version for Netherlands with MAD

Mk 86: Export version for Norway.

Mk 87: Export version for Argentina.

Mk 88: Export version for Germany.

Mk 89: Export version for Nigeria.

Mk 90: Export version for Denmark

HAS 8: Super Lynx upgraded version, with up-rated Rolls-Royce Gem 42-1 engines , BERP rotor blades, thermal imaging sensors and improved electronic warfare systems.

Above:
Westland Lynx HAS Mk 8/Super Lynx
(GKN Westland)

Left:
Westland Lynx HAS.Mk 2 (FN)
(Tim Ripley)

Mk 95: Export Super Lynx for Portugal.
Mk 99: Export Super Lynx for South Korea.
SH-14D: Export version for Netherlands with up-rated Rolls Royce Gem 42-1 engines and full ASW kit.
Super Lynx Series 200/300: Export version with LHTEC CTS800, improved avionics and 'glass' cockpit.

Status
In production.

Operators
Brazil (navy), Denmark (navy), France (navy), Germany (navy), Malaysia (navy), Netherlands (navy), Nigeria (navy), Norway (navy), Pakistan (navy), Portugal (navy), South Korea (navy), UK (navy).

Manufacturer
Westland Helicopters/GKN Westland (UK).

Right:
Westland Lynx HAS Mk 8/Super Lynx
(GKN Westland)

Kaman Seasprite (USA)

Type: Shipborne anti-submarine helicopter

Accommodation: Two pilots, sonar operator, four passengers

Development/History

Making its first flight in 1959, the SH-2F version of the Sea Sprite utility helicopter was selected in 1970 by the US Navy for work on frigates, destroyers and cruisers in the anti-submarine role, under the LAMPS I programme. It lost out to the SH-60 in the LAMPS III contest, and the bulk of the US Navy's fleet have been either relegated to reserve service or retired into storage. A programme to upgraded some surplus US versions to the anti-ship missile-armed SH-2G standard is underway, and the improved helicopter has recently found export success in Australia and New Zealand.

Variants

UH-2B: Shipborne utility helicopter for US Navy.
SH-2D: Initial winner of US Navy Light Airborne Multi-Purpose System (LAMPS) platform contest for embarked small ship helicopter. Powered by two T58-GE-F Powerplants.
SH-2F: Improved version with 101 longer life rotor blades, new search radar and towed MAD boom.
SH-2G Super Seasprite: Advanced version powered by two General Electric T700-GE-401 turboshafts, each rated to 1285 kW (1723 shp). It has improved mission sensors and weapon carriage capabilities.
SH-2G(E): Specialist anti-submarine warfare upgrade for Egypt.
SH-2G(A): Australian export version.
SH-2G(M): Proposed version for Malaysia.

Status

Work continues on SH-2G standard upgrades.

Kaman SH-2F of HSL-34 (Jeremy Flack/API)

Specifications (for SH-2G)

Powerplant
Two General Electric T700-GE-401 turboshafts
Power: 3446 shp (2570 kW)

Dimensions
Length: 40 ft 6in (12.34 m)
Rotor diameter: 44 ft 4 in (13.5 m)
Height: 15 ft 2 in (4.6 m)

Weights
Empty: 9200 lb (4173 kg)
Max T/O: 13,500 lb (6124 kg)

Payload: 4000 lb (1814 kg)

Performance
Max speed: 159 mph (256 kmh)
Range: 478 nm (885 km) with external tanks

Armament
Mk 46, 50 torpedoes; depth charges; 7.62 mm door guns; Penguin Mk 2 Mod 7 radar-guided anti-ship missiles; AGM-65G/M/NZ Maverick air-to-surface guided missile

Operators
Argentina (navy), Australia (navy), Pakistan (navy), New Zealand (air force).

Manufacturer
Kaman Aerospace (US).

Right:
Kaman SH-2F of HSL-34
(Jeremy Flack/API)

Bell Model 47 Sioux (USA)

Type: Light helicopter   **Accommodation:** Two pilots, one passenger

Development/History

One of the first helicopters to go into large-scale production after making its first flight in 1945, some 5,000 have since been built. Although it has now been withdrawn from frontline service by most NATO users, it can still be found in use in obscure corners of Asia and South America.

Variants

H-13 Sioux: Basic US Army and USAF version.
TH-13/HTL-1/2/3/4/5/6/7: US Navy trainer version.
HUL-1//7: US Navy version for training and ice breaking ship operations.
OH-13: Three-seat version.
UH-13: US Navy training version.
AB-47: Italian-built version.
AB 47G-2: UK-built version, designated Sioux AH 1/2.

Status

No longer in production.

Operators

Columbia, Congo (Zaire), Greece (air force), Italy (army), Lesotho, Libya (army), New Zealand, Pakistan (army), Paraguay, Peru (air force/ navy), South Korea (army), Uruguay (navy), Zambia.

Manufacturer

Bell Aircraft Corporation/Bell Helicopter Company (USA), Aqusta (Italy), Westland Helicopters (UK), Kawasaki Heavy Industries (Japan).

Bell 47G operated by the British Army as the AH.1 Sioux   *(API)*

Specifications (for Model 47G-3B-2A)

Powerplant
One Lycoming TVO-435-F1A piston engine
Power: 280 hp (209 kW)

Weights
Empty: 2893 lb (858 kg)
Max T/O: 2950 lb (1338 kg)

Dimensions
Length: 31 ft 7 in (9.6 m)
Rotor diameter: 37 ft 1 in (11.3 m)
Height: 9 ft 3 in (2.8 m)

Performance
Max speed: 105 mph (169 kmh)
Range: 215 nm (397 km)

Bell Model 204/UH-1 Iroquois (Huey) (USA)

Type: Light utility helicopter   **Accommodation:** Two pilots, seven passengers

Development/History

The first of the famous 'Huey' family of helicopters which bore the brunt of the US Army campaign in Vietnam. Several thousand built for the US armed forces from 1956 through to the late 1960s.

Variants

HU-1A: Initial production version for US Army with Lycoming XT53-L-1 turboshaft, rated at 615 kW, (825 shp). Capacity of six passengers. Source of 'Huey' nickname.
HU-1B: Enhanced version with capacity for seven passengers and revised main rotor blades.
UH-1A: Re-designation in 1962 of HU-1A.
UH-1B: Re-designation in 1962 of HU-1B.
UH-1C: Improved version of UH-1B, with T53-L-11 powerplant.
UH-1E: US Marine Corps version with hoist and twin 7.62 mm chin gun turret.
TH-1E: US Marine Corps dual control trainer.
UH-1F: USAF ballistic missile silo security version with General Electric T58-GE-3, rated to 962 kW (1290 shp).
TH-1F: Trainer version of UH-1F.
HH-1K: US Navy rescue version with hoist and T53-L-13 Powerplant, rated to 1044 kW (1400 shp).
UH-1L: US Navy utility version with T53-L-13 powerplant.
TH-1L: US Navy training version with T53-L-13 powerplant.
UH-1M: US Army version with night vision sensor fit.
AB 204: Italian-built version, with powerplant options including T53-GE-3, rated at 962 kW (1290 shp), Textron Lycoming T53-L-11A or Rolls-Royce Gnome H.1200, rated at

Agusta Bell AB 204B   *(Jeremy Flack/API)*

Specifications (UH-1C)

Powerplant
One Textron Lycoming T53-L-11
Power: 1100 shp (820 kW)

Dimensions
Length: 42 ft 7 in (12.98 m)
Rotor diameter: 44 ft (13.41 m)
Height: 12 ft 7.25 in (3.84 m)

Weights
Empty: 5071 lb (2300 kg)

Max T/O: 9500 lb (4309 kg)
Payload: 1361 lb (3000 kg)

Performance
Cruising speed: 148 mph (238 kmh)
Range: 332 nm (615 km)

Armament
Door machine guns; machine gun pods; free-flight rocket pods; Mk 44 torpedoes

Bell Model 204/UH-1 Iroquois (Huey) (USA)

932 kW (1250 shp).

Hkp 3B: Swedish designation of AB 204.

AB 204AS: Italian-built naval version, with T53-GE-3 powerplant, rated at 962 kW (1290 shp)

Fuji-Bell 204B-2: Japanese-built version, also known as Hi'yodori.

Huey Tug: UH-1C with up-rated engines.

RH-2: Research version.

Status

No longer in production.

Operators

Austria, Columbia (air force), Honduras, Indonesia (army), Italy (army), Japan (army), Panama, Paraguay, Somalia, South Korea (army), Spain, Sweden (army), Thailand (army), Turkey (army/ navy), Yemen.

Manufacturer

Bell Aircraft Company/Bell Helicopter Company (USA), Agusta (Italy), Fuji-Bell (Japan).

The Swedish army operates the AB 204 as the Hkp 3B
(Jeremy Flack/API)

Bell Model 205/UH-1 Iroquois (Huey) (USA)

Type: Medium-lift helicopter   **Accommodation:** Two pilots, 12 passengers, six stretchers

Development/History

The first major upgrade of the ever popular 'Huey', which featured a stretched and enlarged cabin to boost carrying capacity. The first of 2500 ordered for the US armed forces entered service in 1963, whilst the last H-model was produced as recently as 1986. It is set to continue in US military service until well into the next century.

Variants

UH-1D: Original US Army version, with Lycoming T53-L-11 powerplant, rated to 820 kW (1100 shp). Capable of carrying 12-14 passengers.

UH-1H: Uprated version for US Army, uprated with T53-L-13 powerplant.

UH-1V: US Army medivac and rescue version with hoist.

CUH-1H: Canadian training version, designated CH-118.

EH-1H: Electronic warfare 'Quick Fix' version.

HH-1H: USAF rescue version.

UH-1HP Huey II: Commercial upgraded version with improved powerplant.

Huey 800: Commercial upgraded version with LHTEC T800 powerplant.

UH-1/T700 Ultra Huey: Commercial upgraded version with General Electric T700-GE-701C powerplant, rated to 1400 kW (1900 shp).

HU-1H: Japanese-built version.

AB 205A: Italian-built military version, designated EM-2, with T53-L-13 powerplant..

AB 205A-1: Improved Italian 204A.

AB 205BG: Prototype Italian version with two Gnome H

Bell UH-1D of German Luftwaffe   *(Tim Ripley)*

Specifications (for UH-1H)

Powerplant
One Textron Lycoming T53-L-13 turboshaft
Power: 1400 shp (1044 kW)

Dimensions
Length: 41 ft 9 in (17.6 m)
Rotor diameter: 48 ft (14.6 m)
Height: 14 ft 5 in (4.4 m)

Weights
Empty: 5210 lb (2363 kg)

Max T/O: 9500 lb (4309 kg)
Payload: 3880 lb (1759 kg)

Performance
Max speed: 127 mph (204 kmh)
Range: 276 nm (511 km)

Armament
Two machine guns in door; optional rockets and machine gun pods

Bell Model 205/UH-1 Iroquois (Huey) (USA)

Bell UH-1H of US Army Reserve
(Tim Ripley)

1200 powerplants.
AB 205TA: Prototype Turboméca Astazous powerplants.
HE.10B: Spanish designation for AB 205.
Advanced 205B: Proposed Japanese upgrade.

Status
No longer in production.

Operators
Argentina (army/navy/air force), Australia (army), Bahrain, Bangladesh, Bolivia, Bosnia-Herzegovina, Brazil (air force), Brunei, Canada, Chile (army/air force), Columbia (air force), Croatia, Dominican Republic, Dubai, El Salvador, Germany (army/air force), Greece (army/air force), Guatemala, Honduras, Indonesia (army), Iran (army, navy, air force), Italy (army), Israel, Jamaica, Japan (army), Jordan, Mexico (air force), Morocco, Myanmar, New Zealand (air force), Oman, Pakistan (army), Panama, Papua New Guinea, Peru (air force/ navy), Philippines, Saudi Arabia (air force), Singapore, South Korea (army/air force), Spain (army), Surinam, Taiwan (army/air force), Tanzania, Thailand (army/navy/air force), Tunisia, Turkey (army/air force), Uganda, UAE (Dubai), USA (army/air force), Uruguay (air force), Venezuela (army/air force), Zambia, Zimbabwe.

Manufacturer
Bell Helicopter Company/Bell Helicopters Textron (USA), Agusta (Italy), AIDC (Taiwan), Dornier (Germany), Fuji-Bell (Japan)

Bell Model 212 UH-1N Iroquois (Twin Huey) (USA)

Type: Medium-lift helicopter   **Accommodation:** Two pilots, 14 passengers

Development/History

A twin-engined 'Huey' was first proposed by Bell Helicopters, Pratt & Whitney Canada and the Canadian Government in 1968. The USAF took delivery of the first aircraft in 1970, and it soon became the standard utility helicopter of the US Marine Corps. Foreign sales followed in large numbers, with more than 882 being built to date.

Variants

UH-1N: Basic US Navy and Marine Corps version.
VH-1N: USAF and US Marine Corps VIP transport.
CUH-135: Canadian version, later designated CH-135 Twin Huey.
Twin Two-Twelve: Civil commercial version.
AB 212: Italian-built utility version, with Pratt & Whitney Canada PT6T-3 Turbo Twin-Pac powerplant.
AB 212ASW: Italian maritime version (described elsewhere).
HU.18: Spanish Army designation.
UN-1N (4BN): Four-blade USMC upgraded version

Status

In production.

Operators

Argentina (army/air force), Austria, Bahrain, Bangladesh, Bolivia, Brunei, Chile (air force), Dominican Republic, Ecuador (air force), El Salvador, Ghana, Greece (army/air force), Guatemala, Guyana, Iran (army/navy), Iraq, Israel, Italy (army/air force), Jamaica, Japan (army), Lebanon, Malta, Mexico (air force), Morocco, Oman, Panama, Peru (air force),

Bell UH-1N of the USAF   *(USAF)*

Specifications (UH-1N)

Powerplant

Two Pratt & Whitney Canada PT6T-3B Turbo Twin Pac
Power: 1800 shp (1342 kW)

Dimensions

Length: 42 ft 4 in (12.9 m)
Rotor diameter: 48 ft 2 in (14.7 m)
Height: 14 ft 10 in (4.53 m)

Weights

Empty: 6097 lb (2765 kg)
Max T/O: 11 200 lb (5080 kg)
Payload: 5000 lb (2268 kg)

Performance

Max speed: 117 mph (189 kmh)
Range: 243 nm (450 km)

Bell Model 212 UH-1N Iroquois (Twin Huey) (USA)

Philippines, Saudi Arabia (air force), Singapore, Slovenia, South Korea (air force), Spain (army/navy), Sri Lanka, Somalia, Sudan, Thailand (air force/navy), Tunisia, Turkey (army), Uganda, Uruguay (air force), Venezuela (navy), Yemen, Zambia, UAE(Dubai), UK (army), USA (navy/marines), United Nations.

Manufacturers

Bell Helicopter Company/Bell Helicopters Textron (USA/Canada), Agusta (Italy)

Bell UH-1N of the USMC
(Tim Ripley)

Bell Model 214 (USA)

Type: Medium utility and transport helicopter

Accommodation: two pilots, 16 passengers

Development/History
The first customer for this high specification version of the 'Huey' was the Imperial Iranian armed forces during the final years of the Shah's regime. Sales have followed to a number of customers who have been prepared to pay premium prices for a superior helicopter.

Variants
214A Isfahan: Iranian-funded development, powered by Textron Lycoming T5508D, rated to 1528 shp (2050 kW).
214B BigLifter: Civilian version.
214C: Search and rescue version.
214ST: Twin-engined version, powered by CT7-2As, with stretched fuselage and composite rotor blades.

Status
No longer in production.

Operators
Brunei, Columbia (air force), Ecuador, Iran (army/navy/air force), Iraq, Oman, Peru (air force), Philippines, Thailand (navy), UAE (Dubai), Venezuela.

Manufacturer
Bell Helicopter Company/Bell Helicopters Textron (USA).

Bell 214 *(Jeremy Flack/API)*

Specifications (for 214ST)

Powerplant
two General Electric CT7-2A turboshafts
Power: 1625 shp (1212kW)

Dimensions
Length: 49ft 3.5 in (15.02 m)
Rotor diameter: 52 ft (15.58 m)
Height: 15f t 10.5 in (4.84 m)

Weights
Empty: 9445 lb (4284 kg)
Max T/O: 7983 lb (9445 kg)
Payload: 7700 lb (3493 kg)

Performance
Cruising speed: 161 mph (259 kmh)
Range: 463 nm (858 km)

Armament
Door-mounted machine guns

Bell Model 412 (USA)

Type: Medium utility and transport helicopter

Accommodation: two pilots, 14 passengers

Development/History

The most recent version of the 'Huey' still manages to find customers around the world. A number of companies are also offering upgrade packages to basic versions.

Variants

412: Basic production version.

412SP: Special Performance version, with improved fuel capacity, known as Arapaho in Norwegian service.

412HP: Emergency medical services version, with improved transmission and PT6T-3BE Twin Pac.

Military 412: Armed version.

412EP: Enhanced performance version with additional fuel. Designated Griffin HT 1 in UK service.

CH-146 Griffon: Canadian military version of 412SP.

NBell-412: Indonesian-built version

AB412 Grifone: Italian-built military version. Designated EM-4 in Italian service.

AB412 CRESO: Italian-built ground surveillance radar platform.

Hkp 11: Swedish designation.

AB 412 EP: Agusta-built version.

Status

In production.

Operators

Bahrain, Botswana, Canada, Columbia (air force), Guatemala, Guyana, Finland (coast guard), Honduras, Indonesia (army), Italy (army/navy/air force), Lesotho, Netherlands (air force),

Bell 412 *(Tim Ripley)*

Specifications (for 412HP)

Powerplant
One Pratt & Whitney Canada PT6T-3D-1 Turbo Twin Pac
Power: 1800 shp (1342 kW)

Dimensions
Length: 42 ft 4 in (12.92 m)
Rotor diameter: 46 ft (14.02 m)
Height: 15 ft (4.57 m)

Weights
Empty: 6654 lb (3018 kg)
Max T/O: 11 900 lb (5397 kg)

Performance
Cruising speed: 140 mph (226 kmh)
Range: 402 nm (745 km)

Armament
Door-mounted machine guns: cannon pods; rocket pods; Air-to-air and air-to-surface missiles

Norway, Peru (air force), Poland (air force), Saudi Arabia (air force), Slovenia, South Korea (air force), Sri Lanka, Sudan, Sweden (army), Thailand (air force/army), Uganda, UAE (Dubai), United Nations, UK (MoD), Zimbabwe.

Manufacturer
Bell Helicopters Textron (USA/Canada), Agusta (Italy), ITPN (Indonesia)

Bell 412 of Dubai Police Air Wing
(Tim Ripley)

Bell Model 206 JetRanger (USA)

Type: Light helicopter **Accommodation:** Two pilots; three passengers

Development/History

The best-selling JetRanger first flew in 1966, and three years later the US Army began to take delivery of the OH-58 variant (see separate entry). It has since been adopted by a large number of armed forces around the world. Some 7700 had been built by 1995.

Variants

Model 205A JetRanger: First production version, with Allison 250-C18 engine, rated to 236.5k W (317 (shp).
Model 206B JetRanger II: Second production version, with Allison 250-C20, rated to 298 kW (400 shp)
Model 206B-3 JetRanger III: Improved version with 250-C20B powerplant.
Model 206 AS: Chilean navy version, armed with torpedoes.
TH-67 Creek: US Army version of JetRanger III, adopted for basic flight training under designation TH206.
Model 206L-1 LongRanger: Stretched fuselage version of JetRanger III.
Model 206L-2 LongRanger II: Improved L-1, with Allison 250-C28B turboshaft, rated to 365 kW (489 shp).
Model 206L-3 LongRanger III: Improved version with Allison 250-C30P turboshaft rated to 485 kW (650 shp).
Model 206L-4 LongRanger IV: Canadian-built version.
Model 206LT TwinRanger: Canadian-built twin-engined version.
Model 206L TexasRanger: Proposed military version of L-2.
Cardoen CB 206L-III: Proposed gunship version for Iraq, built in Chile.
TH-57A SeaRanger: US Navy training version to 206A

Bell 206 in United Nations service in Croatia *(Tim Ripley)*

Specifications (206B-3 JetRanger III)

Powerplant
One Allison 250-C20J turboshaft
Power: 420 shp (313 kW)

Dimensions
Length: 31 ft 2 in (9.5 m)
Rotor diameter: 33 ft 4 in (10.2 m)
Height: 9 ft 6 in (2.9 m)

Weights
Empty: 1625 lb (737 kg)
Max T/O: 3200 lb (1451 kg)
Payload: Under-slung 1500 lb (680 kg)

Performance
Max speed: 140 mph (225 kmh)
Range: 395 nm (732 km)

Armament
Door guns; torpedoes.

standard.

TH-57B SeaRanger: US Navy training version to 206B standard.

TH-57C SeaRanger: US Navy training version to Jet Ranger III standard.

AB 206A-1: Italian-produced military version to 206A standard, designated ERI-3 by Italian military.

AB206A-2: Italian-produced military version to 206B standard, designated ERI-2 by Italian military.

AB206C-1: Italian-modified A-1s upgraded to A-2 standard with -C20 engines.

Hkp 6A: Swedish designation of Italian-produced 206A.

HR.12A: Spanish designation of AB 206A-1.

Zafar 300: Iranian-produced version of 206B-1.

Status

In production.

Operators

Austria, Bangladesh, Brazil (navy), Brunei, Cameron, Chile (army/navy), Columbia (air force), Cyprus, Croatia, Ecuador(air force), Greece (army/air force), Guatemala, Guyana, Jamaica, Israel, Iran (army/navy), Italy (army), Libya (army), Malta, Mexico (air force), Morocco, Oman, Pakistan (army), Peru(army/navy/air force), Saudi Arabia (air force), Slovenia, South Korea (navy), Sri Lanka, Sweden (army/navy), Tanzania, Taiwan (air force), Thailand (army), Turkey (army), Uganda, UAE(Dubai), USA (army/navy), United Nations, Venezuela (army/national guard), Yemen.

Bell 206L-4 LongRanger 4
(Bell Helicopters)

Manufacturer

Bell Helicopter Company/Bell Helicopters Textron (USA/Canada), Agusta (Italy), Cardoen Industries (Chile)

Bell Model 206/OH-58 Kiowa (USA)

Type: Light observation and utility helicopter

Accommodation: Pilot, co-pilot side-by-side, three passengers

Development/History

The US Army bought some 2000 versions of the OH-58 Kiowa from 1969 onwards to fly scout missions with specialist equipment fitted. The basic design has since undergone a number of upgrades to enhance its battlefield survivability.

Variants

OH-58A: Original US Army scout version.
OH-58B: Export version for Austrian Army.
OH-58C: Upgraded US Army version with flat glass canopy and Allison. T63-A720 turboshafts, rated to 313 kW (420 shp).
COH-58A: Canadian version to OH-58A standard, later re-designated CH-136 Kiowa.
Model 206B-1 Kiowa: Australian produced version, later renamed Kalkadoon.

Status

No longer in production.

Operators

Austria, Australia (army/navy), Canada, USA (army).

Manufacturer

Bell Helicopter Company/Bell Helicopters Textron (USA), Commonwealth Aircraft Company (Australia).

US Army OH-58A Kiowa *(Jeremy Flack/API)*

Specifications (for OH-58A)

Powerplant
One Allison T63-A-700 turboshaft
Power: 317 shp (236.5 kW)

Dimensions
Length: 32 ft 3.5i n (9.84 m)
Rotor diameter: 35 ft 4 in (10.77 m)
Height: 9 ft 6.5 in (2.91 m)

Weights
Empty: 1583 lb (713 kg)
Max T/O: 3000 lb (1361 kg)

Performance
Cruising speed: 122 mph (196 kmh)
Range: 260 nm (481 km)

Bell Model 406/OH-58D Kiowa Warrior (USA)

Type: Light armed reconnaissance helicopter

Accommodation: Two pilots side-by-side

Development/History

The 'ultimate' version of the OH-58, the Kiowa Warrior boasts an impressive weapon and sensor fit to allow it to operate alongside the AH-64 Apache as part of joint air attack teams. The Army Helicopter Improvement Program (AHIP) began in 1981, and the first helicopters entered service in 1985.

Variants

OH-58D Kiowa Warrior: US Army armed Scout version.
Multi-Purpose Light Helicopter: US Army modification including folding rotor blades and tail to allow transport in C-130 transport aircraft.
Prime Chance: Code-name for first aircraft fitted with Hellfire and Stinger missiles for shipping escort duties in Middle East in 1987.
MH-58D/406C Combat Scout: Saudi Land Forces version. Also features provision for GIAT 20 mm cannon but no mast-mounted sight.
OH-58X: Stealth technology demonstrator.

Status

In production.

Operators

Saudi Arabia (army), Taiwan (army), USA (army)

Manufacturer

Bell Helicopters Textron (USA).

Bell OH-58D Kiowa Warrior   *(Bell Helicopter Textron)*

Specifications

Powerplant

One Allison T703-AD-700 turboshaft
Power: 650 shp (485 kW)

Dimensions

Length: 34 ft 4 in (10.5 m)
Rotor diameter: 35 ft (10.7 m)
Height: 12 ft 10 in (3.9 m)

Weights

Empty: 3045 lb (1381 kg)

Max T/O: 5500 lb (2495 kg)
Warload: 2000 lb (907 kg)

Performance

Max speed: 147 mph (237 kmh)
Range: 250 nm (463 km)

Armament

Stinger air-to-air missiles; AGM-114 Hellfire laser-guided anti-tank missiles; machine gun pods; free-flight rocket pods

Bell Model 209/AH-1F/G Huey Cobra (USA)

Type: Attack helicopter   **Accommodation:** Pilot, gunner in tandem cockpit

Development/History

Bell Helicopters first produced a gunship version of the Huey in 1965 as a private venture. Its distinctive tandem seating and nose turret have since been copied by attack helicopter designers around the world. Some 1000 G-models were bought by the US Army, and it proved very effective when used in action during the later years of the Vietnam war. The need to counter massed Soviet armoured formations during the Cold War led to a series of upgrading programmes to provide the Cobra with the capability to fire TOW wire-guided anti-tank missiles. Sensor upgrades improved the performance at night and in bad weather. Israeli, Iranian and Turkish forces have used TOW-armed Cobras in combat in the Middle East. US Army late-model Cobras were used in the 1991 Gulf War, and in conflicts in Somalia, Haiti and Bosnia.

Variants

Model 209: Original prototype.
AH-1G: Original US Army gunship version, with T53-L-13 turboshaft rated to 1044 kW (1400 shp).
TH-1G: Dual control trainer version.
AH-1E: Enhanced Cobra armament version with TOW missiles.
AH-1P: TOW missile armed version.
AH-1Q: Upgraded version to allow TOW missile carriage.
AH-1R: Upgraded version with T53-L-703 powerplant.
Improved AH-1S: US Army common upgraded standard for its G/Q models, with T53-L-703 powerplant.
Production AH-1S: New-build versions to AH-1S standard. Up-gunned version has 20 mm cannon nose turret.

US Army AH-1G   *(Jeremy Flack/API)*

Specifications (for AH-1F)

Powerplant
One Textron Lycoming T53-L-703 turboshaft.
Power: 1800 shp (1342 kW)

Dimensions
Length: 53 ft 1 in (16.18 m)
Rotor diameter: 44 ft (13.41 m)
Height: 13f t 5 in (4.09 m)

Weights
Empty: 6598 lb (2993 kg)

Max T/O: 10 000 lb (4536 kg)

Performance
Cruising speed: 141 mph (227 kmh)
Range: 274 nm (507 km)

Armament
Four hard points; eight TOW wire-guided anti-tank missiles; free -flight rockets; M197 20 mm cannon in nose turret; 30 mm grenade launcher in nose turret.

AH-1F: Re-designation and upgrade of US Army S/F/P/E model Cobras, features flat cockpit glass, nose TOW sight and T53-L-703 powerplant. Current in-service version.
Advanced AH-1J/Model 309 King Cobra: Experimental version with single Lycoming T-55-L-7C powerplant.

Status
No longer in production.

Operators
Bahrain, Israel, Japan (army), Jordan, Pakistan (army), South Korea (army), Thailand (army), Turkey (army), United Nations.

Manufacturer
Bell Helicopter Company/Bell Helicopters Textron (USA), Fuji-Bell (Japan).

Right:
AH-1G Huey Cobra of the Maryland National Guard
(Jeremy Flack/API)

Bell Model 209/AH-1W Super Cobra (USA)

Type: Attack helicopter   **Accommodation:** Pilot, co-pilot gunner in tandem

Development/History

US Marine Corps requirements for a twin-engined gunship to allow safe over sea operations led to the fielding of the AH-1J from 1971 onwards. Iran ordered an improved version but this was abandoned after the fall of the Shah in 1979. The US Marine Corps took over the programme which led to the 'Whisky' version. It saw action during the 1991 Gulf War, claiming hundreds of kills on Iraqi tanks with its laser-guided Hellfire missiles.

Variants

AH-1J Sea Cobra: US Marine Corps version with two Pratt & Whitney Canada T400-CP-400 turboshafts, rated to 1342 kW (1800 shp) each.

AH-1J International: Export version of AH-1J.

AH-1T Improved Sea Cobra: Upgraded AH-1J for US Marines with improved T400-WV-402 powerplants, each rated at 1469 kW (1970 shp).

AH-1W Super Cobra: Basic US Marine Corps version with improved T700-GE-401 powerplants, each rated at 1186 kW (1723 shp).

Cobra Venom: Proposed UK version.

AH-1W (4BW): Proposed upgrade for US Marine Corps, providing four main rotor blades and weapon system improvements.

AH-1RO: Romanian-produced version, with customised weapon system.

Model 309 King Cobra: Experimental upgrade with two engines and improved weapons system.

Model 249: Experimental four-blade version.

Bell AH-1W Cobra   *(Bell Helicopter Textron)*

Specifications (AH-1W)

Powerplant
two General Electric T700-GE-401 turboshafts
Power: 3446 shp (2370 kW)

Dimensions
Length: 45 ft 6 in (13.9 m)
Rotor diameter: 48 ft (14.6 m)
Height: 13 ft 6 in (4.1 m)

Weights
Empty: 10 200 lb (4627 kg)
Max T/O: 14 750 lb (6690 kg)

Warload: 4552 lb (2065 kg)

Performance
Max speed: 173 mph (278 kmh)
Range: 365 nm (587 km)

Armament
One three-barrel M197 20 mm gun in nose turret; four hard points; TOW wire-guided anti-tank missiles; Hellfire laser guided anti-tank missiles; AIM-9L Sidewinder air-to-air missiles; gun pods; cluster bombs; free-flight rocket pods

Status
In production.

Operators
USA (marines), Thailand (army),Turkey (army)

Manufacturer
Bell Helicopter Company/Bell Helicopters Textron (USA), IAR SA Brasov (Romania).

Bell AH-1W Cobra
(Bell Helicopter Textron)

Bell/Boeing V-22 Osprey (USA)

Type: Tilt-rotor transport   **Accommodation:** Two pilots, crew chief; 24 troops

Development/History

This revolutionary aircraft has gone through a prolonged development phase but has now progressed to production, with the first examples being delivered in 1999. The Osprey uses its rotors to take off vertically, and they then rotate to provide the power for horizontal flight. Current plans call for some 452 to be purchased by the US Marines to replace their CH-46 assault helicopters. The first unit, HMT-204 'The White Knights', is scheduled to become operational at MCAS Cherry Point, North Carolina, by 2001. The USAF has a requirement for 50 Ospreys for special operations missions to be in service by 2005. The US Navy wants 48 Ospreys for combat search and rescue. Low rate initial production began in 1997 at five aircraft a year, rising to eight in 2000, with a decision on full production due that same year.

Variants

V-22 EMD: Engineering and manufacturing development aircraft.
MV-22B: US Marine Corps assault production version.
SV-22A: Proposed initial US Navy anti-submarine warfare version.
CV-22B: USAF special operations production version.
HV-22B: US Navy combat search and rescue production version.
Bell-Boeing 609: Civilian passenger/VIP transport tilt rotor, built to a smaller scale.

Status

In production.

98

Bell Boeing V-22 Osprey   *(Bell Boeing)*

Specifications (V-22B)

Powerplant

Two Allison T406-AD-400 turboshafts
Power: 12 300 shp (9172 kW)

Dimensions

Length: 57 ft 4 in (17.5 m)
Rotor diameter: 38 ft (11.6 m) each
Height: 17 ft 4 in (5.28 m)

Weights

Empty: 31 886 lb (14 463 kg)
Max T/O: 55 000 lb (24 947 kg)

Payload: 20 000 lb (9072 kg)

Performance

Max speed: 115 mph (185 kmh) in helicopter mode; 316 mph (509 kmh) in fixed wing mode
Range: 1200 nm (2224 km)

Armament

Door-mounted machine guns; maritime versions may be adapted to carry torpedoes and depth charges

Operators
US (navy/marines/air force).

Manufacturer
Bell Helicopters Textron and
Boeing Helicopters (USA).

Bell Boeing V-22 Osprey
(Bell Boeing)

Boeing CH-47 Chinook (USA)

Type: Heavy-lift helicopter   **Accommodation:** Two pilots, crew chief, 55 troops, 24 stretchers

Development/History

The 'mighty' Chinook first flew in 1961 to fulfil a US Army requirement for a heavy-lift helicopter. Viewed by the US Army as a 'flying truck', it proved its worth in Vietnam supporting air mobile troops and flying supplies and artillery pieces to remote jungle fire bases. The large under-slung load capacity of the Chinook soon led it to being nicknamed 'Hooks' by US troops. Some 354 A-models were built for use during the Vietnam War, and more orders soon followed. A constant upgrade programme has significantly improved the capability of the US Army's Chinooks over the ensuing decades. Just under 500 were in service with the US Army, US Army Reserve and National Guard in 1997.

During the 1991 Gulf War CH-47Ds played a key role moving the air mobile forces of the 101st Airborne Division deep behind Iraqi lines. They also opened the way for US peacekeeping force to enter Bosnia in 1996 by lifting pontoon bridge sections into position across the Sava River. Foreign customers have also found the Chinook much to their liking, and sales have been brisk both from the main plant in Philadelphia and other licence production lines. Iran, Italy, Japan and the United Kingdom have been the largest customers for the Chinook, Britain using its aircraft extensively in the Falklands, Northern Ireland, the 1991 Gulf War and Bosnia. Iran found them invaluable during the 1980-88 war against Iraq, whilst Italy operated its helicopters firstly in Somalia in 1993, and then during the evacuation of its citizens from Albania during the 1997 civil war.

Following Britain's example of using the Chinook to move

Boeing CH-47D   *(Tim Ripley)*

Specifications (for CH-47D)

Powerplant
Two Textron Lycoming T55-L-712 turboshafts
Power: 6000 shp (4474 kW)

Dimensions
Length: 51 ft (15.5 m)
Rotor diameter: 60 ft (18.3 m) each
Height: 18 ft 11 in (5.8 m)

Weights
Empty: 26 918 lb (12 210 kg)
Max T/O: 54 000 lb (24 494 kg)
Payload: 27 082 lb (12 284 kg)

Performance
Max speed: 177 mph (285 kmh)
Range: 613 nm (1136 km)

Armament
Door machine guns

its air mobile brigade, the Netherlands has ordered Chinooks to provide mobility for its new rapid reaction force. The US Army use their Chinooks for special forces operations, with night vision devices and in-flight refuelling equipment fitted to allow low-level penetration behind enemy lines at night. Britain's Royal Air Force is also procuring a version with similar capability for long range combat search and rescue missions.

Boeing's Chinook won the battle for international orders against Sikorsky's Sea Stallion, with more than 1087 built, or ordered, for the US Army and export by 1997.

Variants

CH-47A: Original US Army version, with T55-L-5 powerplants, rated to 1641 kW (2200 shp).
CH-47B: Uprated US army version with T55-7C turboshafts, rated to 2125 kW (2850 shp) and increased rotor diameter.
CH-47C: Further improved US Army version with T55-L-11A turboshafts, rated to 2796 kW (3750 shp), and extra fuel capacity.
CH-47D: US Army version with T55-L-712 turboshafts for better performance and triple-lift hook for improved handling of under-slung loads.
CH-147: Canadian version to CH-47C standard.
HT.17: Spanish version to CH-47C standard.
Chinook HC 1: British version to CH-47C standard, but with triple-hook capacity.
Chinook HC 1B: British version retrofitted with glass fibre blades.
Chinook HC 2: British version to CH-47D standard.

Boeing CH-47D *(Tim Ripley)*

Boeing CH-47 Chinook (USA)

Chinook HC 3: British version to MH-47E standard.
MH-47D Special Operations aircraft: Interim upgrade for US Army special operations until fielding of MH-47E..
MH-47E: Special forces version with in in-flight refuelling, night flying capability and T55-L-712 SS engines, each rated to 3264 kW (4378 shp).
Model 414: Export model to CH-47C standard.
International Chinook: Export model to CH-47D standard.
CH-47C Plus: Italian-built version with T55-I-412E powerplants and composite blades.
CH-47J: Japanese-built version to CH-47D standard.
BV234MLR: Civilian version.
ICH CH-47D: Improved Cargo helicopter upgrade for US Army, possibly to be designated CH-46F.
Advanced Chinook: Proposed version with 5000 shp (3729 kW) class engines, redesigned rotors and additional fuel.

Status

In production.

Operators

Argentina (air force), Australia (army), Egypt, Greece (army), Iran (army/air force), Italy (army), Japan (army/air force), Morocco, Netherlands, Singapore, South Korea (army), Spain (army), Taiwan, Thailand (army), UK (air force), USA (army).

Manufacturer

Vertol Aircraft Corporation/Boeing Vertol/Boeing Helicopters (USA), Kawasaki Heavy Industries (Japan), Elicotteri Meridionali/Agusta (Italy).

Boeing CH-47 HC.Mk 2   *(Tim Ripley)*

Boeing CH-47 HC.Mk 2

(Tim Ripley)

Boeing 107/CH-46 Sea Knight (USA)

Type: Medium-lift helicopter   **Accommodation:** Two pilots, crew chief, 25 troops

Development/History

The cambered rotor-bladed Vertol Model 107 made its first flight in 1958 and entered service with the US Marine Corps in 1964. Nicknamed the 'Frog', it saw extensive service as an assault helicopter during the Vietnam War. Subsequent operations in Grenada, the Persian Gulf , Somalia, Liberia and Haiti have seen the CH-46 in the centre of the action. An upgrade programme kept the aircraft flying through the 1970s, 80s and 90s as the mainstay of the Marine Corps' embarked helicopter fleet. The Pentagon is keen to replace the ageing, and increasingly unreliable, CH-46 with the Osprey tilt rotor. Delays in the V-22 programme mean the 'Frog' will have to soldier on into the 21st century.

US Navy fleet support squadrons are large users of the CH-46, operating from shore bases or supply ships. Foreign exports have been small, with Japanese production lines being the main centre of activity. One of the more famous exploits of the aircraft was its use by the Swedish Navy to hunt Soviet submarines in the Baltic Sea during the 1980s.

Variants

107 Model II: Civilian version.
HRB-1/CH-46A: Original US Marine Corps assault version with two T58-GE-8B powerplants, each rated to 932 kW (1250 shp).
UH-46A: US Navy utility and cargo transport version.
CH-46D: Uprated US Marine Corps version with T58-GE-10 turboshafts.
UH-46D: Uprated US Navy version with T58-GE-10 turboshafts.

Boeing CH-46E Sea Knight   *(Tim Ripley)*

Specifications (for CH-46E)

Powerplant
Two General Electric T58-GE-16 turboshafts
Power: 3740 shp (2788 kW)

Dimensions
Length: 44 ft 10 in (13.7 m)
Rotor diameter: 51 ft (15.5 m) each
Height: 16 ft 8 in (5.1 m)

Weights
Empty: 13 067 lb (5927 kg)

Max T/O: 23 000 lb (10 433 kg)
Payload: 9000 lb (4082 kg)

Performance
Max speed: 159 mph (256 kmh)
Range: 206 nm (383 km)

Armaments
Door machine guns

HH-46D: US Marine Corps rescue version.

CH-46F: Final production version for US Marine Corps, with improved avionics.

CH-46E: Upgrade D- and F-models for US Marine Corps, includes glass fibre rotor blades, improved avionics and T58-GE-16 powerplants.

VH-46F: VIP version for US Marine Corps.

KV-107 II/IIA: Japanese-built utility version, exported to Saudi Arabia.

Hkp 4: Swedish designation for KV-107.

CH-113 Labradors: Canadian search and rescue version.

CH-113A Voyageur: Canadian army version.

Status

No longer in production.

Operators

Canada, Japan (army/navy/air force), Sweden (navy), Saudi Arabia (air force), USA (navy/marines).

Manufacturer

Vertol Aircraft Corporation/Boeing Vertol/Boeing Helicopters (USA), Kawasaki Heavy Industries (Japan).

Boeing UH-46D Sea Knight
(Tim Ripley)

Boeing/Sikorsky RAH-66 Comanche (USA)

Type: Reconnaissance/attack helicopter

Accommodation: two pilots in tandem

Development/History

The US Army's much troubled scout helicopter replacement programme has received significant funding, but as yet production is still uncertain. Boeing and Sikorsky won the LHX contract to replace the Cobra, OH-6 and OH-58 in 1991, their first prototype flying in 1996. They have been contracted to supply six aircraft for testing to the US Army by 2002 under a $1.699 billion contract. The second aircraft is to fly in 1998.

The Comanche has a number of unique features, including a bearingless main rotor and shrouded tail rotor. It is the first helicopter to be developed using 'stealth' technology to minimise its radar cross-section, heat signature and engine noise.

Variants

Nil.

Status

In pre-production.

Operators

US (army).

Manufacturer

Boeing Helicopters and Sikorsky Aircraft (USA).

Boeing/Sikorsky RAH-66 Comanche   *(Boeing Sikorsky)*

Specifications (for RAH-66)

Powerplant
Two LHTEC T800/LHT-801 turboshafts
Power: 2688 shp (2004 kW)

Dimensions
Length: 43 ft 4 in (13.2 m)
Rotor diameter: 39 ft (11.9 m)
Height: 11 ft 1 in (3.4 m)

Weights
Empty: 7749 lb (3515 kg)
Max T/O: 10 112 lb (4587 kg)
Warload: 2612 lb (1185 kg)

Performance
Max speed: 204 mph (328 kmh)
Range: 1260 nm (2344 km) with external tanks

Armament
Under development

Boeing/Sikorsky RAH-66 Comanche

(Boeing Sikorsky)

Boeing OH-6 Cayuse/MD500/MD530 (USA)

Type: Light utility helicopter   **Accommodation:** One or two pilots, four passengers

Development/History

The OH-6 Cayuse was developed by the Hughes Helicopter Inc for the US Army's Light Observation Helicopter (LOH) requirement in the early 1960s. Soon nicknamed the 'Loach', it saw active service in Vietnam in large numbers. Hughes, and later McDonnell Douglas, have continued to develop and upgrade the basic design, with more than 4600 having being built by 1997.

Variants

Model 269/300C Osage: Forerunner of 500 series, which lacks enclosed rear fuselage. Military versions designated TH-55. Schweizer Aircraft have since developed the design.

OH-6A (Model 369M) Cayuse: Original US Army light observation helicopter, known as the Loach.

OH-6B: Re-engined version with T63-A-720 powerplant, rated to 313.32 kW (420 shp).

OH-6C: Proposed five-bladed version with improved Allison 25-C20 engine, rated at 298 kW (400 shp). Commercial derivatives designated Model 500D and E.

OH-6J: Japanese-built version to OH-6A standard.

MH-6B: Special forces version.

MH-6C: Special forces version.

EH-6B: Special forces command post/electronic warfare version.

AH-6C: Special forces attack version.

Hughes 500: Civil version of the OH-6A/Model 369 with Allison 250-C18A turboshaft, rated to 236.5 kW (317 shp).

Model 500C: Export version modified for 'hot-and-high' operation.

Boeing MD500 in Israeli service   *(IDF Spokesman)*

Specifications (for Model 500E)

Powerplant
One Allison 250-C20B turboshaft
Power: 450 shp (335.6 kW)

Dimensions
Length: 23 ft (7.01 m)
Rotor diameter: 26 ft 5 in (8.05 m)
Height: 8 ft 9 in (2.67 m)

Weights
Empty: 1445 lb (655 kg)
Max T/O: 3000 lb (1361 kg)

Payload: (530F) 2000 lb (907 kg)

Performance
Max speed: 152 mph (282 kmh)
Range: 233 nm (431 km)

Armament
TOW wire-guided anti-tank missiles; Stinger air-to-air missiles; 30 mm cannon pod; 7.62 mm machine gun pod; free-flight rocket pods; 40 mm grenade launcher; Mk 44 or 46 torpedoes

108

Model 500M Defender: Commercial version of OH-6A.

OH-6D: Japan-built version based on up-engined Hughes 500, five-bladed main rotor and T-tail.

NH500M: Italian-built version based on up-engined Hughes 500.

Model 500M/ASW: Export version for Spain with MAD Boom.

Model 500MD Defender: Military version with armour and infra-red exhaust suppression.

Model 500D Scout Defender: Armed reconnaissance version.

Model 500MD/ASW Defender: Maritime version with search radar and MAD boom.

Model 500MD/TOW Defender: Anti-tank missile armed version.

Model 500MD/MMS-TOW Defender: Anti-tank missile version with mast-mounted sight.

Model 500MD Quiet Advanced Scout Defender: Four-bladed version with noise suppression.

Model 500MD Defender II: Armed version with quiet slow turning four-bladed rotor.

An OH-6 of the Danish army (API)

109

Boeing OH-6 Cayuse/MD500/MD530 (USA)

Model 500E: Revised version with pointed nose, improved tailplane and Allison 25-C20B powerplant.

NH-500E: Italian-built version of 500E.

Model 500MG Defender: Specialist military version of Model 500E.

Model 520MK Black Tiger: Korean-built military version.

MD530F Lifter: Five-bladed main rotor fitted with pointed nose, powered by Allison 250-C30 turboshaft, rated to 317 kW (425 shp).

EH-6E: Special forces command post/electronic warfare version with Allison 250-C30 powerplant.

MH-6E: Special forces version with Allison 250-C30 powerplant.

AH-6F: Special forces attach version Allison 250-C30 powerplant.

MD530MG Defender: Military version with Allison 250-C30 powerplant.

MD530 Nightfox: Night attack version with improved sensors and powerplant.

MD530MG Paramilitary Defender: Specialist version powerplant for police and border patrol.

MD530FF Lifter/MH-6H: Special forces version to MD530MG standard, with glass cockpit and 'people plank'.

AH-6G: Special forces attack version to MD530 standard.

MH-6J: Special forces version with improvements to MH-6H.

AH-6J: Special forces attack similar to MH-6H standard.

MD530N on test at Mesa, Arizona (API)

Status
In production.

Operators
OH-6
Brazil (air force), Japan (army), Taiwan (air force).

MD500
Argentina (army/air force), Bolivia (air force), Columbia (air force), Costa Rica, Croatia, Cyprus, Denmark (army), El Salvador, Finland, Greece (air force), Indonesia (air force), Israel, Italy (air force), Kenya, Mauritania, Mexico (air force), North Korea, South Korea (army/navy), Taiwan (army).

MD530
Chile (army), Columbia, Mexico (air force).

Manufacturers
Hughes Tool Company/Hughes Helicopter Inc/McDonnell Douglas Helicopter Company/Boeing Helicopters (USA), Breda Nardi/Agusta (Italy), Kawasaki Heavy Industries (Japan), Korean Air (South Korea), RACA (Argentina).

OH-6A Cayuse

(API)

Boeing MD 520N/Explorer (USA)

Type: Light utility helicopter   **Accommodation:** One or two pilots, six passengers

Development/History

The NOTAR is a revolutionary tail-rotorless helicopter concept, which has been under development since 1981. As yet it has not been officially adopted by a military user, although US Army special forces are understood to have used NOTAR versions.

Variants

OH-6A NOTAR: Experimental version, first ever NOTAR helicopter.
MD520N: Experimental version with NOTAR rotorless tail, five-bladed main rotor and Allison 250-C20R-2 turboshaft, rated to 335.7 kW (450 shp).
MD Explorer: Twin-engined NOTAR version. Military version called Combat Explorer.
MD600N: Wide-body single-engined NOTAR version. Previously designated MD630N.
MD900: Eight-seat version of Explorer.
MH-6N/AH-6N: Suspected US special forces NOTAR versions.

Status

In production.

Operators

Nil.

Manufacturer

Hughes Helicopter Inc/McDonnell Douglas Helicopter Company/Boeing Helicopters (USA).

The revolutionary Boeing Combat Explorer is reported to be in service with the US Army Special Forces.
(Boeing)

Specifications (for MD Explorer)

Powerplant

Two Pratt & Whitney Canada PW 2068B turboshafts
Power: 1258 shp (938 kW)

Dimensions

Length: 32 ft 4 in (9.86 m)
Rotor diameter: 33 ft 10 in (10.34 m)
Height: 12 ft (3.66 m)

Weights

Empty: 3215 lb (1458 kg)

Max T/O: 2699 lb (5950 kg)
Payload: Under-slung 3000lb (1361 kg)

Performance

Max speed: 172 mph (278 kmh)
Range: 374 nm (602 km)

Armament

AGM-114 Hellfire laser guided anti-tank missiles; machine gun pods; free-flight rocket pods

Boeing AH-64 Apache (USA)

Type: Attack helicopter   **Accommodation:** Pilot (rear), co-pilot/gunner (front)

Development/History

After the successful combat debut of the Cobra in Vietnam, the US Army began formulating requirements in the early 1970s for advanced attack helicopters. Bell Helicopters and Hughes Helicopter Inc were selected to develop competing designs and the latter company was declared the winning contender in 1976, although it was not until 1982 that the contract was issued for the first batch of heavily-armed and armoured AH-64A Apaches. Hughes was bought by McDonnell Douglas in 1984, just as the first Apache was being delivered. Since then the US Army has received some 821 A-models, and more than 100 have been sold to export customers.

The AH-64A showed its potential during NATO Reforger exercises during the late 1980s, but it was not until the 1989 US operation to seize Panama that the Apache first saw action.

In the 1991 Gulf War the Apache showed its full potential by flying deep strike missions behind Iraqi lines. A US Army task force used Apaches to fire the first missiles of Operation Desert Storm, destroying a key Iraqi radar site. Supporting the Coalition ground assault, Apache helicopters accounted for more than 500 Iraqi tanks, 120 APCs, 30 air defence systems, 120 artillery pieces, 325 other vehicles, 10 radars, 50 bunkers, 10 helicopters and 10 aircraft on the ground. Eight AH-64s were hit by enemy fire, but only one was shot down, with its crew surviving. Israeli forces have used the Apache extensively against Islamic guerrillas in southern Lebanon, and on a number of occasions they have employed Hellfire missiles to 'surgically' assassinate key enemy commanders.

Boeing AH-64A Apache of Royal Netherlands Air Force   *(Boeing)*

Specifications (for AH-64A)

Powerplant
Two General Electric T700-GE-701 turboshafts
Power: 3392 shp (2530 kW)

Dimensions
Length: 51 ft (15.5 m)
Rotor diameter: 48 ft (14.6 m)
Height: 12 ft 7 in (3.8 m)

Weights
Empty: 11 225 lb (5095 kg)
Max T/O: 21 000 lb (9525 kg)

Warload: n/a

Performance
Max speed: 227 mph (365 kmh)
Range: 260 nm (482 km)

Armament
One 30 mm M230 Chain Gun; AGM-114 Hellfire laser and millimetre radar guided anti-tank missiles; Mistral, Stinger or Starstreak/Helistreak air-to-air missiles; free-flight rockets

Boeing AH-64A Apache
(Boeing)

Boeing AH-64 Apache (USA)

The intimidating presence of low-flying Apache helicopters in Bosnia from 1996 onwards was considered by US Army commanders to be instrumental in the success of their peacekeeping mission.

The US Army is upgrading its Apache fleet by introducing the Longbow millimetric radar and new radio frequency guided version of the Hellfire missile, which effectively allows for very long range engagements to be fought at night and in bad weather. All the US Army fleet will be modified to allow use of the mast-mounted Longbow radar, but only some 227 radar sets are being purchased. The Netherlands and Britain are the first export customers for the Longbow Apache. To prepare for deployment of the highly capable AH-64D, the Dutch have already received a number of old US Army A-models for use until new build machines are ready. Britain is setting up its own production line to produce its WAH-64Ds, which will feature unique engines, weapon systems and defensive aids – the first helicopter is due to make its premier flight in March 1998.

Variants

YAH-64/Hughes Model 77: Experimental version.
AH-64A: Basic US Army version.
AH-64B/G: Proposed PAH version for German army.
AH-64D Longbow: Improved millimetric radar equipped version.
WAH-64D: UK-built Longbow version with Rolls-Royce/Turboméca RTM322 engines.
AH-64C: US Army versions upgraded to allow installation of Longbow radar. Now to be designated D-models

Boeing AH-64D Longbow Apache   *(Boeing)*

Petan (Cobra): Israeli name.
Sea Apache: Proposed naval version.

Status
In production.

Operators
Egypt (air force), Greece (army), Israel, Saudi Arabia (army), Netherlands (air force), UAE (Abu Dhabi), UK (army), USA (army).

Manufacturers
Hughes Helicopter Inc/McDonnell Douglas Helicopter Company/Boeing Helicopters (USA), Westland Helicopter (UK).

Boeing AH-64D
Longbow Apache
(Boeing)

Sikorsky S-58 Choctaw/Wessex (USA)

Type: Medium-lift helicopter   **Accommodation:** Two pilots, optional crew chief, 16 troops

Development/History

The first versions of the S-58 first flew in 1954, and the US armed forces operated large numbers until the UH-1 Huey entered service in the 1960s. The British-built version, the Wessex, also saw extensive service. Westland improved the Sikorsky single piston-engined design by installing single- and then twin-turboshafts. Users are now withdrawing them from service, although Uruguay has recently bought up surplus British machines.

Variants (still in service)

Wessex HC 2: RAF utility and rescue version. Also operated by Uruguay.
Wessex HC 5: RAF transport and support helicopter.
Wessex HCC 4: RAF Royal Flight VIP version.
Wessex 60: Rescue version used by Uruguay.
CH-34: Transport version.
UH-34D: Transport version.
S-58T: Twin-turboshaft engine-powered version.

Status

No longer in production.

Operators

Argentina (air force), UK (air force), Uruguay (navy), Laos, Taiwan (army) Thailand (air force), Turkey (air force).

Manufacturers

Sikorsky Aircraft (USA), Westland Helicopters (UK).

Westland Wessex HC.Mk 5   *(Tim Ripley)*

Specifications (for Wessex HC 2)

Powerplant
Two Bristol Siddeley Gnome Mk 110/111 turboshafts
Power: 2700 shp (2014 kW)

Dimensions
Length: 48 ft 4 in (14.7 m)
Length: 55 ft 10 in (17 m)
Rotor diameter: 62 ft (18.9 m)
Height: 16 ft 10 in (5.1 m)

Weights
Empty: 8304 lb (3767 kg)
Max T/O: 1350 lb (6123 kg)
Payload: 8000 lb (3628 kg)

Performance
Max speed: 140 mph (226 kmh)
Range: 214 nm (396 km)

Armament
7.62 mm door guns

Sikorsky S-61/SH-3 Sea King (USA)

Type: Medium-lift/naval helicopter

Accommodation: Two pilots, (SH-3) two sonar operators, 26 troops

Development/History

This Sikorsky design made its first flight in 1959, and the American company made several hundred for the United States Navy during the 1960s. The SH-3 proved a very sound maritime helicopter, and NATO navies ordered it in large numbers from American and local production lines.

Westland Helicopters in Britain began to develop its own versions from 1966, including anti-submarine, assault, airborne early warning and search and rescue. Production continued until the mid-1990s, with more than 300 being built for domestic and export markets.

Variants

Y/XSS-2: Prototype versions.

HSS-2/SH-3A: Original US Navy production version for anti-submarine warfare (ASW), powered by T-58-GE-8B turboshafts rated at 937.5 kW (1250 shp), fitted with dipping sonor and capable of carrying torpedoes or nuclear depth charges.

CH-3A/B: Utility version without ASW equipment for US Navy and USAF.

HH-3A: US Navy combat search and rescue version, featuring extra fuel tanks and Minigun armament.

NH-3A: Experimental versions with turbojets and wings.

RH-3A: US Navy mine-sweeping version.

V-3A: US Marine Corps version for Presidential transport.

SH-3D: Improved US Navy ASW version with T58-GE-10 engines and improved mission systems. Licence-built in UK, Italy and Japan.

VII-3D: US Marine Corps version for Presidential transport

Sikorsky S-3G   *(US Navy)*

Specifications (for SH-3H Sea King)

Powerplant
Two General Electric T58-GE-10 turboshafts
Power: 2800 shp (2088 kW)

Dimensions
Length: 54 ft 9 in (16.7 m)
Rotor diameter: 62 ft (18.9 m)
Height: 15 ft 6 in (4.7 m)

Weights
Empty: 11 865 lb (5382 kg)
Max T/O: 20 500 lb (9300 kg)

Payload: 8000 lb (3630 kg)

Performance
Max speed: 166 mph (267 kmh)
Range: 542 nm (1005 km)

Armament
Mk. 44, 46, 50, A244/S, Sting Ray torpedoes; Mk 11 depth charges; Mk 57 and Lulu nuclear depth charges; Sea Eagle, AM39 Exocet, Metre Mk 2 anti-ship missiles; GAU-2 7.62 mm Mini door pods; machine guns.

with T58-GE-10 powerplant.

SH-3G: US Navy improvement of D-model with extra cargo and passenger carrying capacity.

SH-3H: US Navy improvement of D-model with improved mission systems for ASW work.

UH-3H: US Navy utility version without ASW mission equipment.

SH-3D-TS: ASW version.

SH-3H AEW: Spanish navy airborne early warning version with Searchwater radar.

S-61A: Export version for Denmark to SH-3A standard.

AS-61A-4: Search and rescue export version for Malaysia, known as Nuris.

S-61D-3: Brazilian export version to SH-3D standard, later upgraded to SH-3H standard.

S-61D-4: Argentinean export version to SH-3D standard.

Italian-built versions

ASH-3D: Naval version, with T58-GE-100 engines rated to 1125 kW (1500 shp), ASW mission equipment and equipped to fire Exocet and Marte Mk 2 anti-ship missiles.

ASH-3H: ASW version with improved mission equipment.

AS-61-TS: VIP transport version, designated ASH3D/TS.

AS-61A-4: Export utility version with ASH-3D powerplant.

Canadian-built versions

CHSS-2/CH-124A: ASW version to SH-3D standard.

CH-124B/C: Upgraded version with improved mission systems.

Sikorsky SH-3G

(US Navy)

Westland Sea King HC.Mk 4 'Junglie'

(Royal Marines)

Westland Sea King HC.Mk 4 'Junglie'

(Tim Ripley)

Japanese-built versions

S-61B: ASW version to SH-3A, later a S-61B-2 with improved mission systems was fielded to SH-3H standard.
S-61A/AH: Utility, Antarctic survey and rescue version.

British-built versions

Sea King HAS 1: ASW version with Rolls-Royce Gnome H1400 turboshafts rated to 1050 kW (1400 shp).
Sea King HAS 2: Improved ASW version with uprated Gnome H1400-1s.
Sea King HC 4: Assault and troop transport version.
Sea King HAS 5: Improved ASW version with new radar and mission systems.
Sea King HAS 6: Improved ASW version.
Sea King HAR 3: Search and rescue version for RAF.
Sea King HAR 3A: Improved search and rescue version for RAF.
Sea King HAR 5: Royal Navy designation for its search and rescue version.
Sea King Mk 4X: UK Ministry of Defence trails version.
Sea King Mk 41: Export version of Germany for search and rescue.
Sea King Mk 42: Export version for India to HAS 1 standard.
Sea King Mk 42A: Export version for India to HAS 2 standard.
Sea King Mk 42B: Export version for India with uprated Gnome H140-1T powerplants.
Sea King Mk 42C: Export version for India to HAR 3 standard.
Sea King Mk 43/A/B: Export version to Norway for search

Westland Sea King HC.Mk 5 'Junglie' *(Tim Ripley)*

Sikorsky S-61/SH-3 Sea King (USA)

and rescue.

Sea King Mk 45/A: Export version to Pakistan to HAS 12 standard.

Sea King Mk 47: Export ASW version for Egypt to HAS 2 standard.

Sea King Mk 48: Export rescue version for Belgium to HAR 3 standard.

Sea King Mk 50/A: Export version for Australia to HAS 2 standard.

Sea King AEW 2A: Airborne early warning version with Searchwater radar.

Sea King AEW 7: Improved airborne early warning version with upgraded Searchwater radar.

Commando Mk 1 (Sea King Mk 70): Assault and troop transport version for Egypt.

Commando Mk 2 (Sea King Mk 72): Assault and troop transport version for Egypt.

Commando Mk 2A (Sea King Mk 92): Assault and troop transport version for Qatar.

Commando Mk 2C (Sea King Mk 92): VIP version for Qatar.

Commando Mk 2E (Sea King Mk 73): Electronic warfare version for Egypt.

Commando Mk 3 (Sea King Mk 74): Naval version for Qatar, fitted to fire Exocet missiles.

Status

No longer in production

Operators

Argentina (navy), Australia (navy), Belgium, Brazil (navy),

Sea King HC.Mk 4 'Junglie' over Bosnia   *(LA (Phot) Terry Morgan)*

Canada, Denmark (air force), Egypt, Germany (navy), India (navy), Iraq, Iran, Italy (navy/air force), Japan (navy), Malaysia (air force), Norway, Pakistan (navy), Peru (navy), Qatar, Saudi Arabia (air force), Spain (navy), Thailand (navy), Venezuela (army), UK (navy/air force), USA (navy).

Manufacturer

Sikorsky Aircraft (USA), Agusta (Italy), Westland Helicopters (UK), Mitsubishi Heavy Industries (Japan), United Aircraft (Canada).

Westland Sea King HC.Mk 4 'Junglie' in service with the Royal Navy

(Media Production Cell/LAND)

Sikorsky S-61N-1 Silver (USA)

Type: Passenger transport helicopter   **Accommodation:** Two pilots, 30 passengers

Development/History

A development of the Sea King largely for the civil market, this version has been employed by a number of military users for troop transport and rescue work. Civil operators have also chartered them to military customers in the Middle East and the Falklands.

Variants

S-61L: Civil version
S-61NR: Export search and rescue version for Argentina.
AS-61A-1: Italian-made export version for Malaysia.

Status

No longer in production.

Operators

Argentina(air force), Malaysia (air force), UK (MoD), United Nations.

Manufacturer

Sikorsky Aircraft (USA), Agusta (Italy).

Sikorsky S-61N-1 Silver

Specifications (for S-61N)

Powerplant

Two General Electric CT58-140-1 turboshafts
Power: 3000 shp (2236 kW)

Dimensions

Length: 72 ft 10 in (22.2 m)
Rotor diameter: 62 ft (18.9 m)
Height: 17 ft (5.2 m)

Weights

Empty: 12 510 lb (5674 kg)
Max T/O: 22 000 lb (9980 kg)
Payload: 7850 lb (3560 kg)

Performance

Max speed: 146 mph (235 kmh)
Range: 430 nm (796 km)

Sikorsky S-61/HH-3 (USA)

Type: Medium-lift transport helicopter

Accommodation: Two pilots, 30 troops, 15 stretchers

Development/History

Known as the Jolly Green Giant during the Vietnam War, the HH-3E revolutionised combat search and rescue work by being the first in-service helicopter to employ in-flight refuelling. Eventually superseded by the bigger S-65 series in USAF service, the HH-3 found a niche in maritime rescue work with the US Coast Guard and Italian Air Force.

Variants

CH-3E: USAF utility and drone recovery version.
AS-61R Pelican: Italian-built search and rescue version.
HH-3E Jolly Green Giant: USAF combat search and rescue version with in-flight refuelling.
MH-3E: USAF special forces version with in-flight refuelling.
HH-3F Pelican: US Coast Guard search and rescue version.
VH-3E: USAF VIP transport version.

Status

No longer in production.

Operators

Italian (air force), US (coast guard).

Manufacturer

Sikorsky Aircraft (USA), Agusta (Italy).

US Army HH-3F *(API)*

Specifications (CH-3E)

Powerplant
Two General Electric T58-GE-5 turboshafts
Power: 3000 shp (2236 kW)

Dimensions
Length: 57 ft 3 in (17.4 m)
Rotor diameter: 62 ft (18.9 m)
Height: 18 ft 1 in (5.5 m)

Weights
Empty: 13 225 lb (6010 kg)
Max T/O: 22 050 lb (10 000 kg)
Payload: 5000 lb (2270 kg)

Performance
Max speed: 162 mph (261 kmh)
Range: 404 nm (748 km)

Armament
Door machine guns

Sikorsky S-65A/CH-53 Sea Stallion (USA)

Type: Heavy-lift transport helicopter

Accommodation: Two pilots, crew chief, 37 troops, 24 stretchers

Development/History

Sikorsky's big lifter first flew in 1964, and was quickly adopted by the US Marine Corps as its heavy assault transport. Some 124 D-models were bought by the Marine Corps, and have remained in service through to the 1990s. The USAF adopted the aircraft as its principal long-range special operations and combat search and rescue helicopter, instigating several upgrades to maintain its deep penetration capabilities.

Variants

CH-53A: Original USMC version powered by General Electric T64-GE-16 turboshafts.

TH-53A: USAF training version similar in capability to CH-53A.

HH-53B/C: USAF combat search and rescue version with in-flight refuelling probes.

CH-53C: USAF rescue version with out in-flight refuelling probe.

CH-53D: Improved USMC version with uprated T64-GE-413 engines, each rated at 2927 kW (3925 shp).

RH-53D: US Navy minesweeper, powered by two T64-GE-415s each rated at 3266 kW (4380 shp).

MH-53J Pave Low III: USAF special operations version, fitted with in-flight refuelling, night vision equipment and terrain following radar and powered by two T64-GE-7A each rated to 2935 kW (3936 shp).

S-65C-2/0: Austrian export versions built to CH-53C standard, later sold to Israel.

S-65C-3: Israeli export version similar to USAF HH-53Cs.

Sikorsky/VFW-Fokker CH-53G Sea Stallion serving with the United Nations Special Commission in Iraq after the Gulf War (Tim Ripley)

Specifications (for CH-53A)

Powerplant
Two General Electric T64-GE-16 turboshafts
Power: 5124 shp (6870 kW)

Dimensions
Length: 67 ft 2 in (20.47 m)
Rotor diameter: 72 ft 3 in (22.02 m)
Height: 24 ft 11 in (7.6 m)

Weights
Empty: n/a
Normal T/O: 35 000 lb (15 875 kg)
Payload: External 13 000 lb (5897 kg)

Performance
Max speed: 195 mph (314 kmh)
Range: 257 nm (413 km) with auxiliary tanks

Armament
7.62 mm or 12.7 mm door guns

Sikorsky CH-53D Sea Stallion

(Tim Ripley)

Sikorsky S-65A/CH-53 Sea Stallion (USA)

CH-53 2000: Israeli upgrade also known as Yas'ur 2000, designed to extend life into the next century. Turkey is interested in buying this version.

CH-53G: German-built version.

Status
No longer in production.

Operators
Germany (army), Iran, Israel, USA (air force/navy/marines).

Manufacturer
Sikorsky Aircraft (USA), VFW-Fokker (Germany).

Sikorsky MH-53J
Pave Low
(USAF/DoD)

Sikorsky S-80/CH-53E Super Stallion (USA)

Type: Heavy-lift transport helicopter

Accommodation: Two pilots, crew chief, 55 troops

Development/History

The S-80 series Super Stallion utilizes three engines to make it one of the most powerful heavy-lift helicopters in the world. The US Marine Corps and Navy began taking delivery in 1981, and some 177 were built until production ceased in 1995.

Mine clearing versions used by the US Navy and Japanese Maritime Self-Defence Force are operated from amphibious warfare ships or shore bases.

Variants:

CH-53E Sea Stallion: US Navy and Marine Corps Assault and heavy-lift version.
MH-53E Sea Dragon: US Navy mine-sweeping version.
S-80E: Proposed export version of CH-53E.
S-80M-1: Japanese mine-sweeping version.

Status

No longer in production.

Operator

USA (navy/marines), Japan (navy).

Manufacturer

Sikorsky Aircraft (USA).

Sikorsky CH-53E Sea Stallion

(Tim Ripley)

Specifications (for CH-53E)

Powerplant
Three General Electric T64-GE-416 turboshafts
Power: 13 140 shp (9798 kW)

Dimensions
Length: 73 ft 4 in (22.3 m)
Rotor diameter: 79 ft (24.1 m)
Height: 29 ft 5 in (8.9 m)

Weights
Empty: 33 228 lb (15 072 kg)
Max T/O: 69 750 lb (31 640 kg)
Payload: Under-slung 36 000 b (16 330 kg)

Performance
Max speed: 196 mph (315 kmh)
Ferry Range: 1120 nm (2074 km)

Armament
7.62 mm or 12.7 mm door guns

Sikorsky S-80/CH-53E Super Stallion (USA)

Sikorsky CH-53E Sea Stallion

(Tim Ripley)

Sikorsky MH-53E Sea Dragon
(United Technologies/Sikorsky Aircraft)

Sikorsky MH-53E Sea Stallion
(United Technologies/Sikorsky Aircraft)

Sikorsky S-70/UH-60 Blackhawk (USA)

Type: Medium-lift utility helicopter

Accommodation: Two pilots, crew chief, 14 troops

Development/History

In the early 1970s the US Army began looking for a UH-1 Huey replacement which would take into account many of the lessons learnt from combat helicopters operations in Vietnam. Improved crash worthiness was a major criterion in the design, which first flew in 1974.

The first production version flew in 1978, and soon the UH-60A was in widespread service with the US Army, seeing combat in Grenada in 1983. An improved version capable of lifting a HUMVEE or a 155 mm howitzer under-slung was developed in the late 1980s, eventually being designated the UH-60L. In total the US Army has bought some 1400 against original plans for 2262. Low rate production continues for the US Army and export.

Variants

UH-60A: Original US Army utility version.
UH-60B SOTAS: Proposed ground surveillance radar version.
UH-60L: US Army version with uprated T700-GE-710C engines.
UH-60P: South Korean version to L-model standard.
UH-60Q Dustoff: Proposed Medical evacuation version, with external hoist.
EH-60A Quick Fix: Electronic warfare version.
EH-60C Quick Fix: Improved electronic warfare version.
MH-60A Velcro Hawk: US Army special forces version.
MH-60G: Pave Hawk USAF special forces version with in-flight refuelling.
HH-60G: USAF search and rescue version.
MH-60K: US Army special forces version with in-flight

Sikorsky UH-60L Blackhawk   *(Tim Ripley)*

Specifications (for UH-60A)

Powerplant
Two General Electric T700-GE-700 turboshafts
Power: 3244 shp (2420 kW)

Dimensions
Length: 50 ft (15.3 m)
Rotor diameter: 53 ft 8 in (16.4 m)
Height: 16 ft 10 in (5.1 m)

Weights
Empty: 11 284 lb (5118 kg)
Max T/O: 20 250 lb (9185 kg)

Payload: 8000 lb (3629 kg) underslung

Performance
Max speed: 184 mph (296 kmh)
Range: 319 nm (592 km); 1200 nm (2222 km) with max external fuel

Armament
7.62 mm or 12.7 mm door guns and pods: free-flight rocket pods; AGM-114 Hellfire laser guided anti-tank missiles

Sikorsky S-70 Armed Blackhawk

(United Technologies/Sikorsky Aircraft)

Sikorsky HH-60G Pave Hawk

(United Technologies/Sikorsky Aircraft)

refuelling probe.

MH-60L: US Army special forces version with in-flight refuelling probe and uprated T700-GE-710C engines.

VH-60N: US Presidential transport version.

S-70A-1: Saudi land forces version.

S-70A-1L: Saudi VIP transport/medevac version.

S-70A-5: Philippines export version.

S-70A-9: Australian-assembled version

S-70A-11: Jordanian export version.

S-70A-12: Japanese search and rescue version, designated UH-60J.

S-70A-14: Brunei export version.

S-70A-16: Test bed for Rolls-Royce/Turboméca RTM 332.

S-70A-17: Turkish export versions.

S-70A-19: Westland-produced version, designated WS-70.

S-70A-21: Egypt export version.

S-70A-24: Mexican export version.

S-70A-26: Moroccan export version.

S-70A-27: Hong Kong export version.

S-70C: Chinese export version.

S-70C-2: Rescue version with hoist used by Taiwan and Brunei.

Status

In production.

Operators

Australia (army), Bahrain, Brazil (army), Brunei, China, Columbia (army/air force), Egypt, Israel, Greece (army), Hong Kong, Japan (army/air force), Jordan, Malaysia, Mexico,

Sikorsky UH-60L Blackhawk   *(United Technologies/Sikorsky Aircraft)*

Sikorsky S-70/UH-60 Blackhawk (USA)

Morocco, Philippines (air force), Saudi Arabia (army), South Korea (army), Taiwan (air force), Turkey (army), Thailand (army), USA (army/navy/air force).

Manufacturer
Sikorsky Aircraft (USA), Mitusbishi Heavy Industries (Japan), Westland Helicopters (UK), Hawker de Havilland (Australia), Korean Air (South Korea).

Sikorsky S-70A Blackhawk of Royal Brunei Armed Forces (United Technologies/ Sikorsky Aircraft)

Sikorsky S-70B/SH-60 Seahawk (USA)

Type: Maritime helicopter   **Accommodation:** Two pilots, mission specialist

Development/History

Navalised version of the S-70 series won the US Navy's LAMPS competition with a development contract being issue in 1977. The SH-60B has 83 per cent commonality with the UH-60, but includes many features necessary for operations afloat, including anti-corrosion treatment for the airframe, improved engines and a RAST recovery device to secure the helicopter to a rolling ship deck in heavy seas. The US Navy has continued to develop the basic design, including a anti-submarine version with dunking sonar and a specialist combat search and rescue variant. Moves are now in had to standardise the fleet under the SH-60R programme.

Status

In production.

Variants

SH-60B Seahawk: Original US Navy light multi-purpose system (LAMPS) Mk III frigate and destroyer-borne helicopter, with APS-124 radar, MAD and sonobouy launching systems.

SH-60F Ocean Hawk: Carrier-borne (CV) inner sea zone anti-submarine helicopter, with Bendix dipping sonor and provision for three Mk 50 torpedoes.

S-70B-3/SH-60J: Japanese-built version of SH-60B.

SH-60R: US Navy programme to standardise B, F and H versions.

S-70B-2 RAWS: Australian version with domestically-produced radar, sonobouy and other systems. Also provision for Sea Skua and Penguin radar-guided anti-ship missiles.

Sikorsky S-70B-6 Seahawk of Greek Navy

(United Technologies/Sikorsky Aircraft)

Specifications (for SH-60B)

Powerplant

Two General Electric T700-GE-401C turboshafts
Power: 3800 shp (2834 kW)

Dimensions

Length: 50 ft 0.75 in (15.26 m)
Rotor diameter: 53 ft 8 in (16.36 m)
Height: 17 ft (5.18 m)

Weights

Empty: 13 648 lb (6191 kg)

Max T/O: 21 884 lb (9926 kg)
Payload: n/a

Performance

Max speed: 145 mph (234 kmh)
Range: 50 nm (92.5 km) for 3-hour loiter

Armament

7.62 mm and 12.7 mm door guns; AGM-119B Penguin anti-ship missiles; Mk 46 or Mk 50 torpedoes; free-flight rockets.

Sikorsky S-70B/SH-60 Seahawk (USA)

S-70C(M)-1 Thunderhawk: Taiwanese version of SH-60F. Local conversion to Signals intelligence role has taken place.
HH-60H Rescue Hawk: US Navy specialised combat search and rescue version, with extra armament and night vision systems.
HH-60J Jayhawk: US Coast Guard search and rescue version.
S-70B-6: Greek export version.
S-70B-7: Thai naval version with PT6B-36B engines.
CH-60: Proposed US Navy utility version for support and vertical replenishment.
Maplehawk: Proposed Canadian rescue version.

Operators
Australia (navy), Greece (navy), Japan (navy), Spain (navy), Taiwan (navy), USA (navy/coast guard).

Manufacturers
Sikorsky Aircraft (USA), Mitusbishi Heavy Industries (Japan), ASTA (Australia).

Sikorsky SH-60B Seahawk
(United Technologies/
Sikorsky Aircraft)

Sikorsky SH-60B Seahawk   (United Technologies/Sikorsky Aircraft)

Sikorsky S-76 (USA)

Type: Medium-lift utility helicopter   **Accommodation:** Two pilots, 14 passengers

Development/History

This private venture product has sold well to a number of civil and military customers around the world, but it has not found favour with the US armed forces.

Variants

S-76: Original version powered by Allison 250-C30 turboshafts, rated to 485 kW (650 shp).
S-76 Mk II: Improved version.
S-76 Utility: Basic version.
AUH 76: Armed utility derivative, with provision for anti-armour, rockets and guns.
S-76A/C: Version with 539kW (981 shp) Turboméca Arriel 1S1 powerplant.
S-76B: Production version with PT6B-36A powerplant.
H-76B: Military version of S-76B, with weapons provision.
H-76N: Naval version.
HE.24: Spanish designation.

Status

In production.

Operators

Chile (army), Guatemala, Honduras, Hong Kong, Iraq, Japan, Jordan, Philippines (air force), Spanish (air force), South Korea (army).

Manufacturer

Sikorsky Aircraft (USA) and Daewoo (Korea).

Sikorsky S-76C   *(United Technologies/Sikorsky Aircraft)*

Specifications (for H-76)

Powerplant

Two Pratt & Whitney Canada PT6B-36A turboshafts
Power: 1962 shp (1464 kW)

Dimensions

Length: 44 ft (13.4 m)
Rotor diameter: 44 ft (13.4 m)
Height: 14 ft 5 in (4.4 m)

Weights

Empty: 6641 lb (3012 kg)

Max T/O: 11 700 lb (5307 kg)
Payload: n/a

Performance

Max speed: 178 mph (287 kmh)
Range: 357 nm (661 km)

Armament

7.62 mm, 12.7 mm or 20 mm machine gun pods; Stinger air-to-air missiles; Hellfire laser-guided missiles; TOW wire-guided anti-tank missiles; free-flight rockets

Glossary

AEW Airborne early warning.

ASV Air-to-surface vessel.

ASVW Anti-surface vessel-warfare.

ASW Anti-submarine warfare.

avionics Aviation electronics, such as communications radio, radars, navigation systems and computers.

bearingless rotor Rotor in which flapping lead/lag and pitch change movements are provided by the flexibility of the structural material and not by bearings. No rotor is rigid.

carbonfibre Fine filament of carbon/graphite used as strength element in composites.

CAS Close air support.

CBU Cluster bomb unit.

CFRP Carbonfibre-reinforced plastics.

CO-IN Counter-insurgency.

comint Communications intelligence.

composite material Made of two constituents, such as filaments or short whiskers plus adhesive, forming binding matrix.

databus Electronic highway for passing digital data between aircraft sensors and system processors, usually MIL-STD-1553B or ARINC 419 (one way) and 619 (two way) systems.

derated Engine restricted to power less than potential maximum (usually such engine is flat rated).

DF Direction finder or direction finding.

fenestron Helicopter tail rotor with many slender blades rotating in short duct.

FLIR Forward-looking infra-red.

fly-by-light Flight control system in which signals pass between computers and actuators along fibre optic leads.

fly-by-wire Flight control system with electrical signalling (i.e. without mechanical interconnection between cockpit flying controls and control surfaces).

g Acceleration due to mean Earth gravity (i.e. of a body in free fall), or acceleration due to rapid change of direction of flight path.

GPS Global Positioning System.

gunship Helicopter designed for battlefield attack, normally with slim body carrying pilot and weapon operator only.

hardpoint Reinforced part of aircraft to which external load can be attached, e.g. weapon/tank pylon.

HMD Helmet-mounted display, hence HMS = sight.

hot and high Adverse combination of airfield height and high ambient temperature, which lengthens required take-off distance (TOD).

hp Horsepower.

HUD Head-up display.

IFF Identification friend or foe.

IR Infra-red.

IRST Infra-red search and track.

J-STARS US Air Force/Navy Joint Surveillance Target Attack Radar System in Boeing E-8A.

JTIDS Joint Tactical Information Distribution System.

Kevlar Aramid fibre used as basis of high-strength composite material.

km/h Kilometres per hour.

kN Kilonewtons, the metric unit for measuring power output of jet engine.

knot 1 nm per hour.

kW Kilowatts, the metric unit for measuring power output of a propeller-driven engine.

lb Pounds of static thrust, the measurement of a jet engine's static thrust.

LLTV Low-light TV (thus LLLTV, low-light-level).

low observables Materials and structures designed to reduce aircraft signatures of all kinds.

m metre(s), the metric unit of length.

MAD Magnetic anomaly detector.

MFD Multi-function display.

MMS Mast-mounted sight.

MO Maximum permitted operating Mach number.

mph Miles per hour.

MaxTO Maximum take-off weight.

nm Nautical mile, 1.15152 miles (1.8532 km)

NOE Nap-of-the-Earth (low-flying in military aircraft using natural cover of hills and trees etc).

NVG Night Vision Goggles.

optronics Combination of optics and electronics in viewing and sighting systems.

port Left side, looking forward.

pylon Structure linking aircraft to external load (engine nacelle, drop tank, bomb etc).

radius The distance an aircraft can fly from base and return without intermediate landing.

RAM Radar absorbent material.

rigid rotor see bearingless rotor.

RPV Remotely-piloted vehicle.

SAR i) Search and rescue.
ii) synthetic aperture radar.

shp Shaft horsepower, measure of power transmitted via rotating shaft.

sigint Signals intelligence.

signature Characteristic "fingerprint" of all electromagnetic radiation (radar, IR etc).

single-shaft Gas turbine in which all compressors and turbines are on common shaft rotating together.

SLAR Side-looking airborne radar.

stabiliser Fin (thus, horizontal stabiliser = tailplane).

starboard Right side, looking forward.

t Tonne, 1 Megagram, 1000 kg.

tilt-rotor Aircraft with fixed wing and rotors that tilt up for hovering and forward for fast flight.

T-O Take-off.

ton Imperial (long) ton = 1.016 t or 2240 lb; US (short) ton = 0.9072 t or 2000 lb.

turboshaft Gas turbine in which as much energy as possible is taken from gas jet and used to drive helicopter rotors.

UAV Unmanned air vehicle.

winglet Small auxiliary aerofoil, usually sharply upturned and often sweptback, at tip of wing.

Acknowledgements

I would like to thank the following for their help and advice during the preparation
of this book: Jon Lake; Jennifer at Jane's Library; Peter Donaldson and Ian Parker,
Defence Helicopter Magazine; Peter Felstead, Jane's Intelligence Review; Commander
Ken Jay, Royal Navy, and Pauline Elliott, Centre for Defence and International Security
Studies; Ian Drury, HarperCollins; Nigel Vinsen, Royal United Services Institute; and
Neil Tweedie and Mick Brookes at the Hotel Richmond.

Design: Rod Teasdale
Cover photographs: Peter Foster
Colour reproduction by Colourscan, Singapore
Printed in Italy

First published in Great Britain by HarperCollins*Publishers* in 1998

1 3 5 7 9 10 8 6 4 2
©HarperCollins*Publishers* 1998
ISBN 0 00 472134 9

UK information address:
HarperCollins*Publishers*
77-85 Fulham Palace
Road
Hammersmith
London W6 8JB

US information address:
HarperCollins*Publishers* Inc
10 East 53rd Street
New York
NY 10022